A **STEP-BY-STEP** GUIDE TO THE
EYFS

Linda Tallent and Kate Reed

Featherstone

Published 2010 by A&C Black Publishers Limited
36 Soho Square, London W1D 3QY
www.acblack.com

ISBN 978-1-4081-2896-1

Text © Linda Tallent and Kate Reed
A CIP record for this publication is available from the British Library.

Printed in Great Britain by Latimer Trend and Company Ltd

This book is produced using paper that is made from wood grown in managed, sustainable forests. It is natural, renewable and recyclable. The logging and manufacturing processes conform to the environmental regulations of the country of origin.

To see our full range of titles
visit **www.acblack.com**

Contents

About the Authors

Linda Tallent has many years of experience as an early years teacher. She now works as a Primary Teaching and Learning consultant, providing advice, support and training to early years practitioners, senior managers and local authority officers. Her areas of specialism are Raising Boys' Achievement and Developing the Outdoor Learning Environment. Her work has been recognised and acknowledged nationally. She is co-author of the book *Raising Boys' Achievement: getting it right from the start*, written in collaboration with Gary Wilson.

Kate Reed is a well known nationally recognised expert in the field of Early Education. She has an in depth knowledge of how young children learn. Kate worked as a primary school teacher before working for a Local Authority as an under eights advisor, a registration and inspection officer, training and curriculum manager and education consultant. Since 2005 Kate has worked freelance delivering training and undertaking consultancy work for a wide range of clients.

The purpose of this book is to provide practitioners with support in implementing the EYFS. In her role as a teaching and learning consultant, Linda observed that practitioners were making use of and implementing materials contained in the printed books *Practice Guidance for the Early Years Foundation Stage* (which deals with only one of sixteen commitments) and the *Statutory Framework for the Early Years Foundation Stage* (which covers the legal requirements relating to learning, development and welfare). Practitioners appeared to be unaware that the CD-ROM provided detailed information on how to implement the other fifteen commitments.

A Step-by-step guide to the EYS provides practitioners with a step-by-step guide on how to access the information contained on the CD-ROM and available on the DCSF website: http://**nationalstrategies.standards.dcsf.gov.uk/earlyyears/eyfs**. It summarises the key messages and identifies issues for consideration. The book supports practitioners to reflect upon their practice and provides a framework for further development. The book will also be invaluable to students preparing for a career in early years education.

Introduction

The documents *Curriculum Guidance for the Foundation Stage* (2000), the Birth to Three Matters (2002) framework and the *National Standards for Under 8s Daycare and Childminding* (2003) have been brought together into one publication entitled *The Early Years Foundation Stage* which became statutory from September 2008. The EYFS consists of two documents (*Statutory Framework for the Early Years Foundation Stage* and *Practice Guidance for the Early Years Foundation Stage*), a CD-ROM, a poster and a set of Principles into Practice cards. The four overlying principles of the document are:

- A Unique Child
- Positive Relationships
- Enabling Environments
- Learning and Development.

There are five welfare requirements:

- Safeguarding and Promoting Children's Welfare
- Suitable People
- Suitable Premises, Environment and Equipment
- Organisation
- Documentation

The purpose of the EYFS is to ensure a consistent approach to care and learning from birth to the end of the Foundation Stage. The document focuses on stages of development rather than chronological, age-based teaching and learning.

'The overarching aim of the EYFS is to help young children achieve the five **Every Child Matters** *outcomes of staying safe, being healthy, enjoying and achieving, making a positive contribution, and achieving economic wellbeing.'*
(EYFS Statutory Framework, p7)

The web site **http://www.nationalstrategies.standards.dcsf.gov.uk/earlyyears** provides practitioners with up-to-date information on recent research and publications. The contents of the EYFS CD-ROM can be assessed from this site.

The purpose of this book is to provide practitioners with support in implementing the EYFS. There are a total of 16 commitments. The *Practice Guidance* document provides detailed information on only one commitment (4.4 'Areas of Learning and Development'). The CD-ROM contains most of the information on the other 15 commitments. This book provides practitioners with a step-by-step guide on how to access the information contained on the CD-ROM. It summarises the key messages and identifies issues for consideration. The book supports practitioners to reflect upon their practice and provides a framework for further development with photocopiable self-evaluation checklists.

The book is intended to be kept by your side when you are using the CD-ROM or accessing the website. The following symbols will help guide you through using and understanding the EYFS:

	Follow the arrow and click with your mouse to find out new information		Direct question relating to effective practice
	Identifies key messages. Reflect on whether there are implications for your practice		This page may be photocopied

1 A Unique Child

Theme: A UNIQUE CHILD

> **PRINCIPLE**
> Every child is a competent learner from birth who can be resilient, capable, confident and self-assured.

The four commitments describe how the principle can be put into practice:

1.1 CHILD DEVELOPMENT provides practitioners with information to support their understanding of child development. The commitment emphasises that child development is a continuous process and that not all babies and children mature at the same rate. All areas of development are equally important. The commitment acknowledges that the experiences a child has during its early years strongly influence their future development.

1.2 INCLUSIVE PRACTICE provides practitioners with information and practical advice to support their understanding of inclusion. All children, regardless of race, religion or abilities, have an equal right to be listened to and to be valued in the setting. No child or family should be discriminated against.

1.3 KEEPING SAFE acknowledges that young children are vulnerable. It provides practitioners with advice on how to maintain the balance between being overprotected and allowing children to learn about possible dangers. It encourages practitioners to provide children with advice on how to protect themselves from harm.

1.4 HEALTH AND WELL-BEING acknowledges that children's health is an integral part of their emotional, mental, social, environmental and spiritual well-being. It provides practitioners with advice on how to meet both the emotional and physical needs of babies and children.

The four Principles into Practice cards 1.1, 1.2, 1.3 and 1.4, provide practitioners with information about effective practice and give practical suggestions on how to plan activities that build on children's interests. They encourage practitioners to reflect upon their practice and identify challenges and dilemmas they may meet in their work with young children.

A Unique Child

1.1 Child Development

Action point from Principles into Practice card 1.1

How do you support each child's individual development through the experiences and activities you provide in your setting?

How to use the CD-ROM to support understanding of Child Development

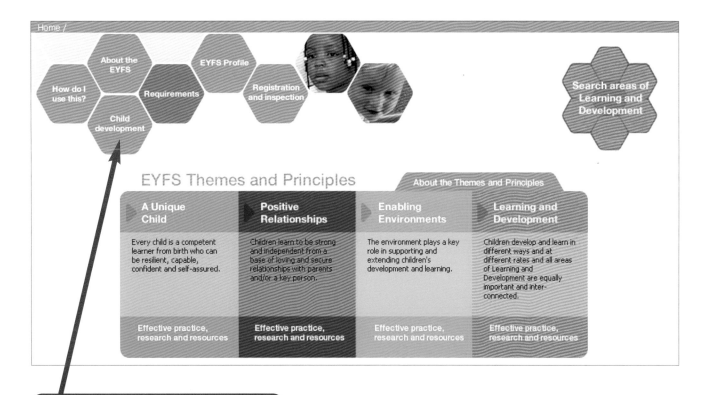

Home /

About the EYFS

EYFS Profile

How do I use this?

Requirements

Child development

Registration and inspection

Search areas of Learning and Development

EYFS Themes and Principles

About the Themes and Principles

A Unique Child	Positive Relationships	Enabling Environments	Learning and Development
Every child is a competent learner from birth who can be resilient, capable, confident and self-assured.	Children learn to be strong and independent from a base of loving and secure relationships with parents and/or a key person.	The environment plays a key role in supporting and extending children's development and learning.	Children develop and learn in different ways and at different rates and all areas of Learning and Development are equally important and inter-connected.
Effective practice, research and resources	Effective practice, research and resources	Effective practice, research and resources	Effective practice, research and resources

Clicking on the Child development hexagon takes you to a screen entitled: Child development overview (see next page)

Child Development Overview

These summaries highlight the more important aspects of child development in each of the six stages of the EYFS. Further information can be found in the Principles into Practice cards, in the Learning and Development sections on the CD-ROM and in the linked Early Support materials which give more detail on the areas of Learning and Development.

Broad phases of development

All children are different and to reflect this age ranges have been overlapped in the EYFS to create broad developmental phases. This emphasises that each child's progress is individual to them and that different children develop at different rates. A child does not suddenly move from one phase to another, and they do not make progress in all areas at the same time. However, there are some important 'steps' for each child to take along their own developmental pathway. These are shown on the areas of Learning and Development in the sections Look, listen and note and Development matters. There are six broad developmental phases.

Birth–11 months

During this period, young children's physical development is very rapid and they gain increasing control of their muscles. They also develop skills in moving their hands, feet, limbs and head, quickly becoming mobile and able to handle and manipulate objects. They are learning from the moment of birth. Even before their first words they find out a lot about language by hearing people talking, and are especially interested when it involves themselves and their daily lives. Sensitive caregiving, which responds to children's growing understanding and emotional needs, helps to build secure attachments to special people such as parents, family members or carers. Regular, though flexible, routines help young children to gain a sense of order in the world and to anticipate events. A wide variety of experience, which involves all the senses, encourages learning and an interest in the environment.

8–20 months

As children become mobile new opportunities for exploration and exercise open up. A safe and interesting environment, with age-appropriate resources, helps children to develop curiosity, coordination and physical abilities. This is a time when children can start to learn the beginnings of self-control and how to relate to other people. In this period children can be encouraged to develop their social and mental skills by people to whom they have a positive attachment. Building on their communication skills, children now begin to develop a sense of self and are more able to express their needs and feelings. Alongside non-verbal communication children learn a few simple words for everyday things and people. With encouragement and plenty of interaction with carers, children's communication skills grow and their vocabulary expands very rapidly during this period.

16–26 months

Children in this phase are usually full of energy and need careful support to use it well. Growing physical strengths and skills mean that children need active times for exercise, and quiet times for calmer activities. Playing with other children is an important new area for learning. This helps children to better understand other people's thoughts and feelings, and to learn how to cooperate with others. Exploration and simple self-help builds a sense of self-confidence. Children are also learning about boundaries and how to handle frustration. Play with toys that come apart and fit together encourages problem solving and simple planning. Pretend play helps children to learn about a range of possibilities. Adults are an important source of security and comfort.

22–36 months

Children's fine motor skills continue to develop and they enjoy making marks, using a variety of materials, looking at picture books and listening to stories, important steps in literacy. Self-help and independence soon emerge if adults support and encourage children in areas such as eating, dressing and toileting. Praise for new achievements helps to build their self-esteem. In this phase, children's language is developing rapidly and many are beginning to put sentences together. Joining in conversations with children is an important way for children to learn new things and to begin to think about past, present and future. Developing physical skills mean that children can now usually walk, climb and run, and join in active play with other children. This is an important time for learning about dangers and safe limits.

30–50 months

An increased interest in joint play such as make-believe, construction and games helps children to learn the important social skills of sharing and cooperating. Children also learn more about helping adults in everyday activities and finding a balance between independence and complying with the wishes of others. Children still need the comfort and security of special people. Close, warm relationships with carers form the basis for much learning, such as encouraging children to make healthy choices in food and exercise. At this stage children are becoming more aware of their place in a community. Literacy and numeracy can develop rapidly with the support of a wide range of interesting materials and activities. Children's language is now much more complex, as many become adept at using longer sentences. Conversations with adults become a more important source of information, guidance and reassurance.

40–60+ months

During this period children are now building a stronger sense of their own identity and their place in a wider world. Children are learning to recognise the importance of social rules and customs, to show understanding and tolerance of others, and to learn how to be more controlled in their own behaviour. Learning and playing in small groups helps to foster the development of social skills. Children now become better able to plan and undertake more challenging activities with a wider range of materials for making and doing. In this phase children learn effectively in shared activities with more able peers and adults. Literacy and problem solving, reasoning and numeracy skills continue to develop. Children's developing understanding of cause and effect is encouraged by the introduction of a wider variety of equipment, media and technologies.

**department for
children, schools and families**

Acknowledgements Disclaimer
00012-2007CDO-EN

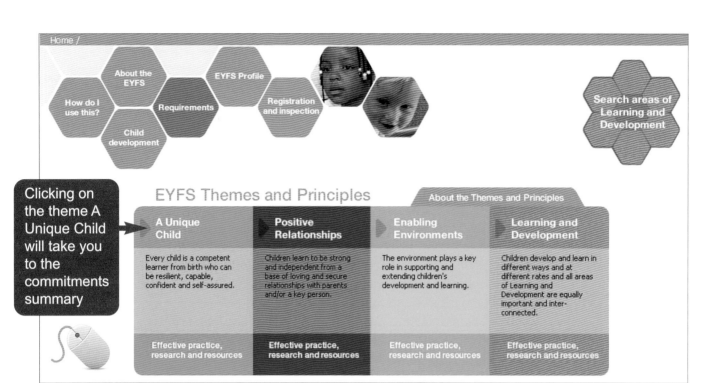

Clicking on the theme A Unique Child will take you to the commitments summary

EYFS Themes and Principles

About the Themes and Principles

A Unique Child	Positive Relationships	Enabling Environments	Learning and Development
Every child is a competent learner from birth who can be resilient, capable, confident and self-assured.	Children learn to be strong and independent from a base of loving and secure relationships with parents and/or a key person.	The environment plays a key role in supporting and extending children's development and learning.	Children develop and learn in different ways and at different rates and all areas of Learning and Development are equally important and inter-connected.
Effective practice, research and resources	Effective practice, research and resources	Effective practice, research and resources	Effective practice, research and resources

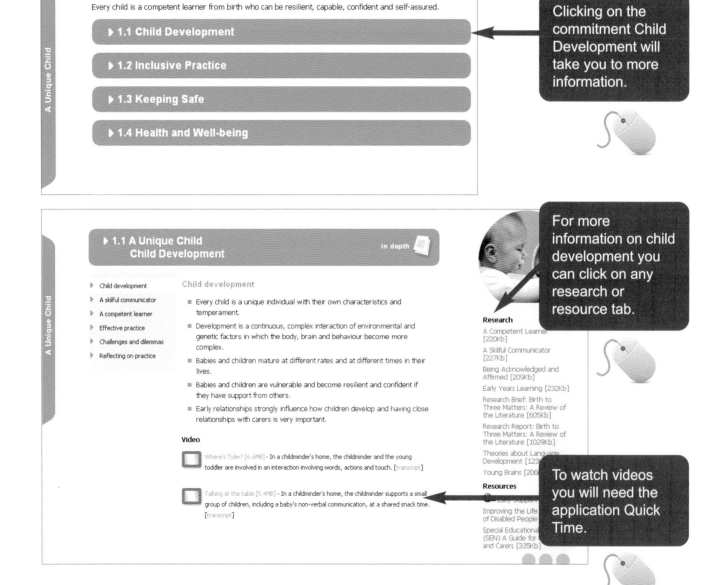

A Unique Child

Every child is a competent learner from birth who can be resilient, capable, confident and self-assured.

▶ **1.1 Child Development**

▶ **1.2 Inclusive Practice**

▶ **1.3 Keeping Safe**

▶ **1.4 Health and Well-being**

Clicking on the commitment Child Development will take you to more information.

▶ **1.1 A Unique Child**
Child Development

in depth

- ▶ Child development
- ▶ A skilful communicator
- ▶ A competent learner
- ▶ Effective practice
- ▶ Challenges and dilemmas
- ▶ Reflecting on practice

Child development

- Every child is a unique individual with their own characteristics and temperament.
- Development is a continuous, complex interaction of environmental and genetic factors in which the body, brain and behaviour become more complex.
- Babies and children mature at different rates and at different times in their lives.
- Babies and children are vulnerable and become resilient and confident if they have support from others.
- Early relationships strongly influence how children develop and having close relationships with carers is very important.

Video

Where's Tyler? [6.6MB] - In a childminder's home, the childminder and the young toddler are involved in an interaction involving words, actions and touch. [transcript]

Talking at the table [5.4MB] - In a childminder's home, the childminder supports a small group of children, including a baby's non-verbal communication, at a shared snack time. [transcript]

Research
A Competent Learner [220Kb]
A Skilful Communicator [227Kb]
Being Acknowledged and Affirmed [209Kb]
Early Years Learning [232Kb]
Research Brief: Birth to Three Matters: A Review of the Literature [605Kb]
Research Report: Birth to Three Matters: A Review of the Literature [1029Kb]
Theories about Language Development [123
Young Brains [206

Resources
Early Support
Improving the Life of Disabled People
Special Educational (SEN) A Guide for and Carers [335Kb]

For more information on child development you can click on any research or resource tab.

To watch videos you will need the application Quick Time.

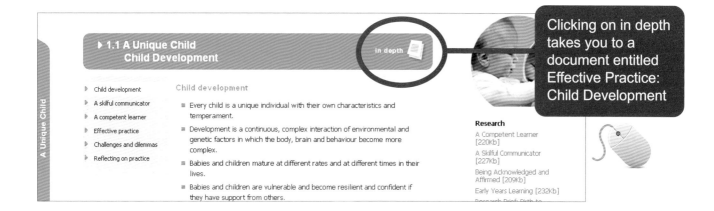

Clicking on in depth takes you to a document entitled Effective Practice: Child Development

The document contains the following:

Key messages (summary)

- **Stages of development in children generally follow a natural sequence. The pace of development will vary from child to child.**

- **A child's development can be affected by external factors.**

- **Each child is affected by their individual circumstances and has a unique story. Practitioners need to acknowledge this and use this knowledge to support their development and learning.**

- **Practitioners need to discuss any concerns about a child's development with parents and if necessary seek help from other professionals.**

- **Children's learning is enhanced by positive interactions with other more able children and adults who skilfully support their learning.**

The document **defines** the following terms:
- Growth
- Development
- Learning.

The document gives **in-depth information** on the following:

Effective practice in relation to Child Development
- Obtain an accurate picture of the child and their family prior to admission and keep clear records which are regularly shared with the family and updated with them.

- Gather information about the child's:
  - Particular needs
  - Family
  - Health
  - Development and learning
  - Wider information.

Developmental stages – Birth to Five

A Unique Child

1.2   Inclusive Practice

Action point from Principles into Practice card 1.2

How do you encourage children to recognise their own unique qualities and the characteristics they share with other children?

How to use the CD-ROM to support understanding of Inclusive Practice

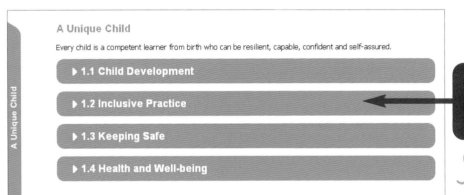

A Unique Child

Every child is a competent learner from birth who can be resilient, capable, confident and self-assured.

▶ **1.1 Child Development**

▶ **1.2 Inclusive Practice**

▶ **1.3 Keeping Safe**

▶ **1.4 Health and Well-being**

> Clicking on the commitment Inclusive Practice will take you to more information.

> For more information on Inclusive Practice you can click on any research or resource tab.

▶ **1.2 A Unique Child**
Inclusive Practice   in depth

- ▶ Children's entitlements
- ▶ Equality and diversity
- ▶ Early support
- ▶ Effective practice
- ▶ Challenges and dilemmas
- ▶ Reflecting on practice

Early support

- It is important to identify the need for additional support as early as possible. Without it children will not get the help they need at the right time, in the way that is right for them.

- Early support for children includes listening to families and taking part in a sensitive two-way exchange of information.

- For children with the most severe and complex additional support needs you need to plan jointly with everyone who is in contact with the child. This will coordinate support and promote learning as effectively as possible.

- Knowing when and how to call in specialist help is one important element of inclusive practice.

Video

 Meeting individual needs [7.3MB] - In the nursery class, the practitioner supports an individual child in his home language while exploring a till and money. [transcript]

Tuning into the child [4.5MB] - In a nursery class, the practitioner leaves the shared snack area to support the particular interests of the child. [transcript]

> To watch videos you will need the application Quick Time.

Research

Research Brief: Early Support: An Evaluation of Phase 3 of Early Support

Research Report: Early Support: An Evaluation of Phase 3 of Early Support

Research Brief: Models of Good Practice in Joined-Up Assessment: Working for Children with 'Significant and Complex Needs' [154Kb PDF]

Research Report: Models of Good Practice in Joined-Up Assessment: Working for Children with 'Significant and Complex Needs'

Research Report: SEN and Ethnicity: Issues of Over- and Under-Representation [245Kb PDF]

Research Report: Special Educational Needs and Ethnicity: Issues of Over- and Under-Representation

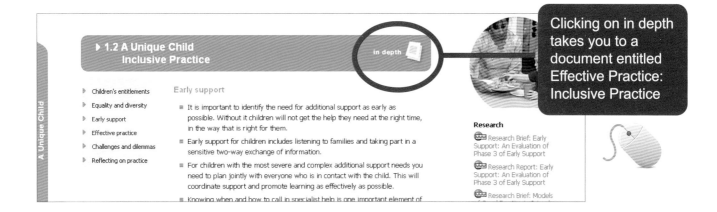

Clicking on in depth takes you to a document entitled Effective Practice: Inclusive Practice

The document contains the following:

Key messages (summary)

● **Inclusion is about attitudes as well as behaviour and practices.**

● **Children are affected by the behaviour of adults and their attitude to diversity.**

● **Practitioners need to embrace the principle of individualised learning and support the development of all children.**

● **Practitioners need to work in partnerships and share information with families. This is particularly important when a child has additional needs.**

● **Systems to track children's development need to be in place. This will support the early identification of children with emerging special educational needs.**

● **Settings should ensure that practitioners have appropriate training to develop their inclusive practice.**

● **Inclusion is not optional, settings have legal responsibilities.**

Providers have obligations under legislation:

● The Race Relations Act makes it a duty to eliminate unlawful racial discrimination [and to], promote equality and promote good relations between people of different racial groups.

● The Disability Discrimination Act expresses a duty not to treat disabled children 'less favourably' than others and to make 'reasonable adjustments' to include them.

● The SEN Code of Practice expresses inclusion as an expectation that practitioners and settings will extend the concept of 'individualised learning' and provide any additional help needed to include and support individual children with special educational needs, using a graduated approach at Early Years Action or Early Years Action Plus (DfES 2001).

The document gives in-depth information on the following:

Why Inclusive Practice is important
- Extending the scope of individualised learning.

Effective practice in relation to Inclusive Practice
- Challenging and changing attitudes – making everyone welcome.

Children from minority ethnic groups
- Settings should:
  - Have a Race Equality Action plan.
  - Have a named member of staff responsible for race equality.
  - Have a commitment to challenging and eradicating racism.
  - Check that resources reflect cultural and ethnic diversity and do not promote negative stereotypes, for example, ensure dolls and puppets have accurate and realistic skin tones, facial features and hair textures.

Children learning English as an additional language
- Practitioners should value this linguistic diversity and provide opportunities for children to develop and use their home language in their play and learning.
- They should actively promote bilingualism and encourage all children to learn some of the languages they hear around them. They should model this themselves – by, for example, greeting children and parents in their home language or asking children how they would say something in their home language.

Children with special educational needs and/or disabilities

Partnership working with parents – tracking development together and sharing information

Getting help when help is needed

Transitions and admissions

The main key message for practitioners is the importance of identifying the need for additional support as early as possible.

Resources

All of Us – Inclusion Checklist for Settings. This checklist can be found on the CD-ROM. It can be accessed by clicking on Enabling Environments then clicking on the commitment 3.3: The Learning Environment. Look on the right hand side of the page – the checklist can be found under the heading 'Resources.'

A Unique Child

1.3 Keeping Safe

Action point from Principles into Practice card 1.3

How do you ensure that children within your setting know what is acceptable and unacceptable behaviour?

How to use the CD-ROM to support understanding of Keeping Safe

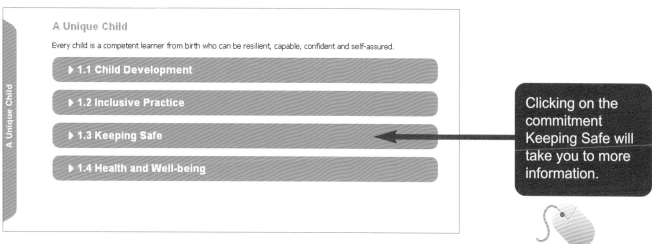

A Unique Child

Every child is a competent learner from birth who can be resilient, capable, confident and self-assured.

▶ **1.1 Child Development**

▶ **1.2 Inclusive Practice**

▶ **1.3 Keeping Safe**

▶ **1.4 Health and Well-being**

Clicking on the commitment Keeping Safe will take you to more information.

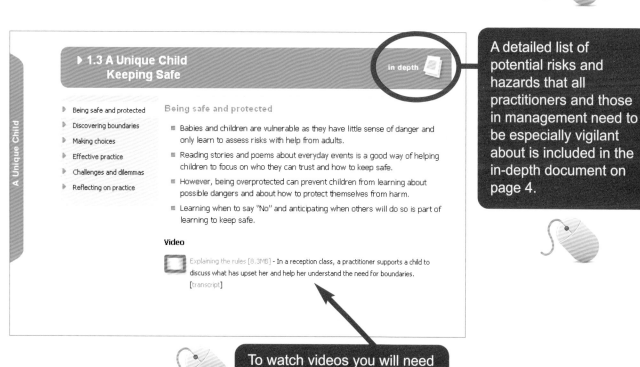

▶ **1.3 A Unique Child Keeping Safe**

in depth

- Being safe and protected
- Discovering boundaries
- Making choices
- Effective practice
- Challenges and dilemmas
- Reflecting on practice

Being safe and protected

- Babies and children are vulnerable as they have little sense of danger and only learn to assess risks with help from adults.
- Reading stories and poems about everyday events is a good way of helping children to focus on who they can trust and how to keep safe.
- However, being overprotected can prevent children from learning about possible dangers and about how to protect themselves from harm.
- Learning when to say "No" and anticipating when others will do so is part of learning to keep safe.

Video

Explaining the rules [8.3MB] - In a reception class, a practitioner supports a child to discuss what has upset her and help her understand the need for boundaries. [transcript]

A detailed list of potential risks and hazards that all practitioners and those in management need to be especially vigilant about is included in the in-depth document on page 4.

To watch videos you will need the application Quick Time.

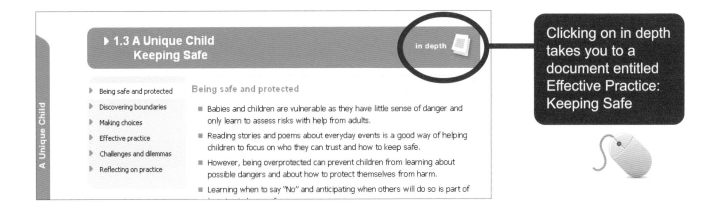

Clicking on in depth takes you to a document entitled Effective Practice: Keeping Safe

The document contains the following:

Key messages (summary)

- **Actively listen to and observe children.**

- **Be aware of any risks, identify and share any concerns.**

- **Keep the setting clean, safe and secure.**

- **Practitioners need to update training regularly.**

- **Relevant documentation must be kept up-to-date.**

- **Ensure premises, equipment and materials are clean, safe and appropriate for the children attending the setting.**

- **Practitioners need to foster children's natural curiosity and exploratory drive and support them to make choices, assess risks and keep themselves safe.**

The document gives in-depth information on the following:

Keeping Safe
- Relates to children's physical and psychological well-being.
- Requires both the people in the setting and the environment itself to offer a safe, familiar context for children to develop, explore and learn, while encouraging curiosity, adventure and independence.
- Requires practitioners to make judgements about the element of risk children are exposed to. The following three factors are central to determining whether or not the level of risk is acceptable or tolerable:
  - the likelihood of coming to harm;
  - the severity of that harm;
  - the benefits, rewards or outcomes of the activity.
- Requires practitioners to maintain continuous risk assessment, but practitioners must also consider children's natural curiosity, their drive to explore and to learn about their world when completing risk assessments.

Effective practice in relation to Keeping Safe

- All adults are alert to potential hazards.
- Practitioners establish effective partnerships with parents, ensuring both children and their parents feel safe and secure and are made welcome in the setting.
- Policies about safety, including those concerned with child protection procedures, are shared with parents.
- This section includes information on how to support children to:
  - Discover their boundaries.
  - Make choices.

Keeping Safe and developmental stages

- This section describes the risks and challenges faced by children at each broad phase of development.

How Keeping Safe relates to specific areas of Learning and Development

- This section outlines how each area of Learning and Development relates to aspects of keeping safe.

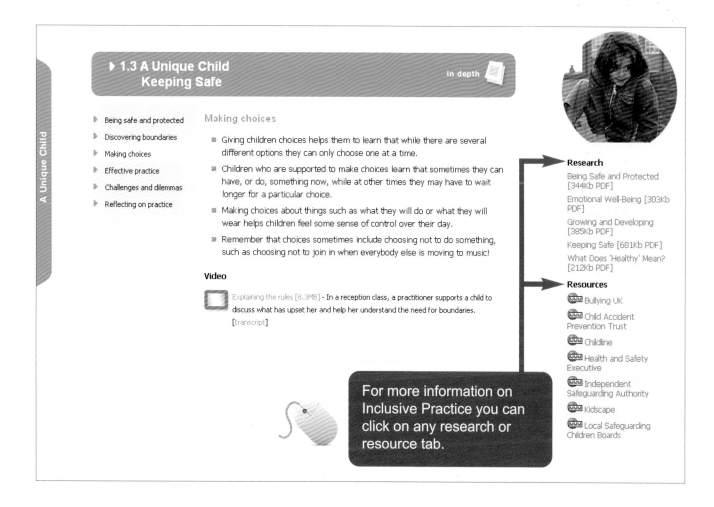

One of the main key messages for practitioners is the importance of supporting children to make choices.

A Unique Child

1.4 Health and Well-being

How to use the CD-ROM to support understanding of Health and Well-being

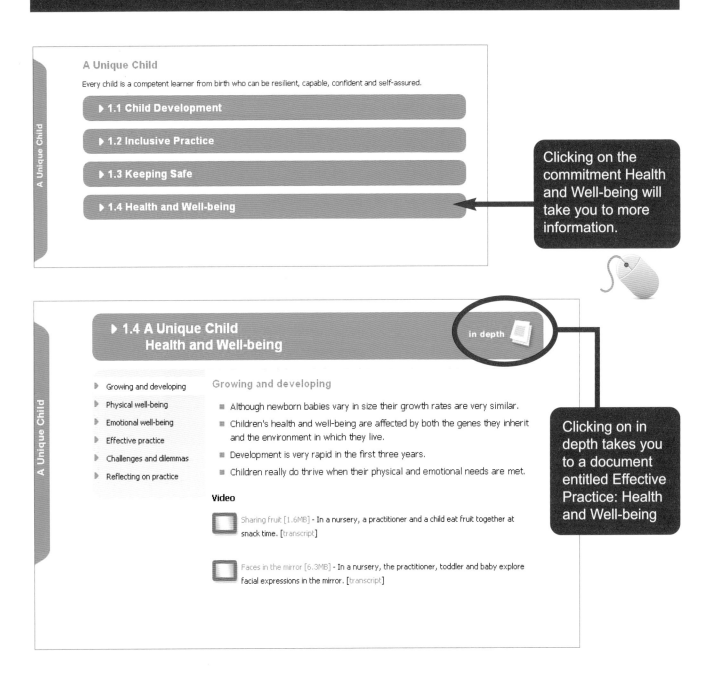

The document contains the following:

Key messages (summary)

- **Children need to know that they are cared for by a key person. This promotes resilience.**

- **To develop, children need a balanced diet and their physical and psychological need to be met. They need an environment that is safe and secure in which they can play and explore.**

- **Children need to have boundaries and routines. They need to be involved in the life of the setting.**

- **Practitioners need to support parents as well as children.**

- **Children's health and well-being are affected when they are in situations of abuse or neglect.**

- **Practitioners need to consider how they meet the additional requirements of children with special needs.**

- **Within each setting there should be a designated person who is trained and is responsible for child protection issues and health and safety.**

- **The wider community should be aware of the importance of the first five years in a child's life.**

- **The setting should develop relationships with other professionals such as health visitors and community paediatricians.**

The document gives in-depth information on the following:

Health and well-being
- Requires that babies and children are cared for by someone who is important to them. This is essential for their physical, social and emotional health and well-being.
- Requires that practitioners enable babies and children to engage in physical play, have a balanced diet and learn about healthy eating. Practitioners should do what they can to protect them from becoming ill, injured or stressed.

Effective practice in relation to Health and Well-being
- Brain development relies on a good diet, both physically and mentally.

Further information on brain development can be found in a document entitled 'Young Brains'. This can be accessed by clicking on A Unique Child commitment 1.1: Child Development. Look on the right hand side of the page – the document can be found under the heading 'Research'.

Physical well-being
- Practitioners working with children need to be aware of health risks to physical development and to be able to find ways of supporting families and young children to overcome these potential hazards.
- Practitioners also promote children's health and well-being when they pay careful attention to hygiene, such as hand washing, sterilising feeding equipment and following practices such as wearing gloves when changing nappies or cleaning up when a child has been ill.
- Practitioners help children to know how to look after themselves by protecting them from too much sun, by providing changes of clothing when they are wet or muddy and wrapping them up warmly for outdoor play. The care practitioners give provides opportunities for shared thinking and conversation that promotes cognitive development.

Emotional well-being

- Practitioners need to find the best ways of offering care, nurture and learning that match with the needs and interests of the individual baby or young child. Being capable of giving this kind of emotional support depends on practitioners being emotionally strong. They too need support and a nurturing work context to enable them to display the degree of commitment this demands.

How health and well-being relates to specific areas of Learning and Development

- This section outlines how each area of Learning and Development relates to aspects of health and well-being.

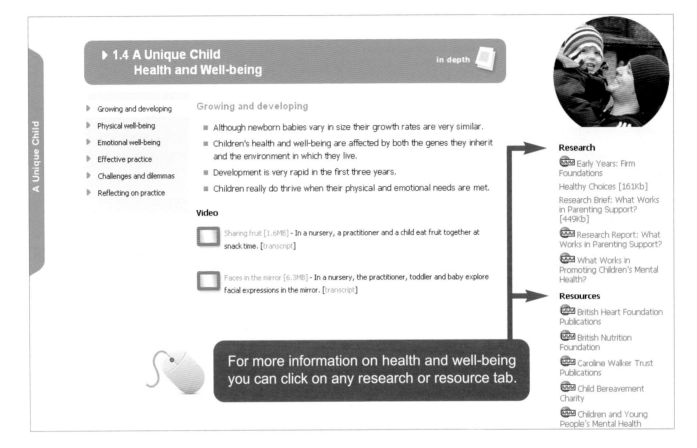

One of the main key messages for practitioners is the importance of fostering the physical, mental and emotional well-being of every child individually.

Further information on supporting children with special needs can be found in a research document entitled 'Early Years Transitions and Special Educational Needs'. This can be accessed by clicking on Enabling Environments commitment 3.4 The Wider Context. Look on the right hand side of the screen, the document can be found under the heading 'Research'.

Further information on supporting children's sense of well-being can be accessed by clicking on Enabling Environments commitment 3.3 The Learning Environment. Next click on the Outdoor Environment in the grey box on the left of the screen. This commitment states that 'being outdoors has a positive impact on children's sense of well-being and helps all aspects of children's development'.

2 Positive Relationships

Theme: POSITIVE RELATIONSHIPS

PRINCIPLE

Children learn to be strong and independent from a base of loving and secure relationships with parents and/or a key person.

The four commitments describe how the principle can be put into practice:

2.1 RESPECTING EACH OTHER emphasises the need for practitioners to help children to value who they are and to respect other children who may come from different ethnic backgrounds or have different abilities or personalities. It provides practitioners with advice on how to support children to develop positive friendships. It stresses the importance of children being able to recognise and name emotions. This will help them to deal with difficult or stressful events. The commitment highlights the importance of developing professional relationships which focus on respecting and recognising the contribution made by everyone in the workplace.

2.2 PARENTS AS PARTNERS acknowledges that parents are children's first and most enduring educators. It provides practitioners with advice on how to welcome and value all 'families' by creating a welcoming atmosphere which values diversity. The commitment emphasises the importance of parents contributing to the child's learning and development record.

2.3 SUPPORTING LEARNING acknowledges the importance of building respectful and caring relationships with all children and families. It provides practitioners with advice on how to listen to, rather than talk at, children. The commitment stresses the importance of building on children's interests and using them as vehicles for learning. Children need to be encouraged to make connections in their learning and to reflect on their learning.

2.4 KEY PERSON acknowledges the importance of settings identifying a key person who has special responsibilities for working with a small number of children. Their role is to meet the needs of each child in their care and respond sensitively to their feelings, ideas and behaviour. It provides practitioners with advice on how to create records of the child's development and progress. The commitment stresses the importance of involving parents, the child, the key person and other professionals in creating and sharing individual records.

The four Principles into Practice cards 2.1, 2.2, 2.3 and 2.4, provide practitioners with information about effective practice and give practical suggestions on how to build relationships with parents, children and other professionals. They encourage practitioners to reflect upon their practice and identify challenges and dilemmas they may meet in their work with young children and their families.

Positive Relationships

2.1   Respecting Each Other

Action point from Principles into Practice card 2.1

Do you make time to listen to parents, to learn about their feelings and discuss any concerns?

How to use the CD-ROM to implement the commitment 'Respecting Each Other'

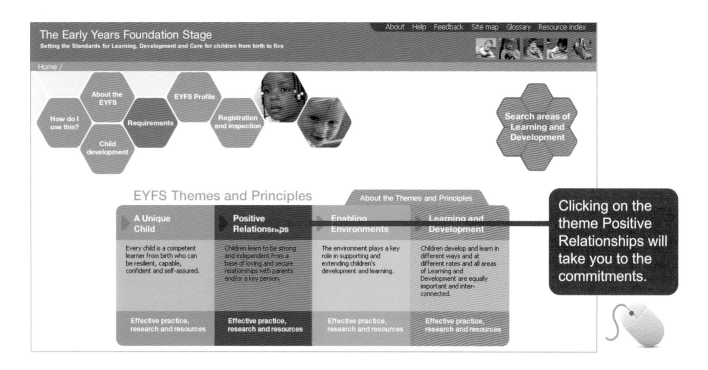

Clicking on the theme Positive Relationships will take you to the commitments.

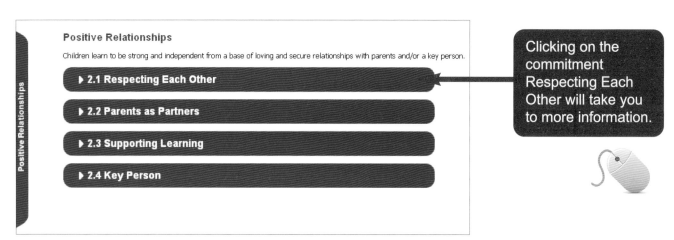

Positive Relationships

Children learn to be strong and independent from a base of loving and secure relationships with parents and/or a key person.

▶ **2.1 Respecting Each Other**

▶ **2.2 Parents as Partners**

▶ **2.3 Supporting Learning**

▶ **2.4 Key Person**

Clicking on the commitment Respecting Each Other will take you to more information.

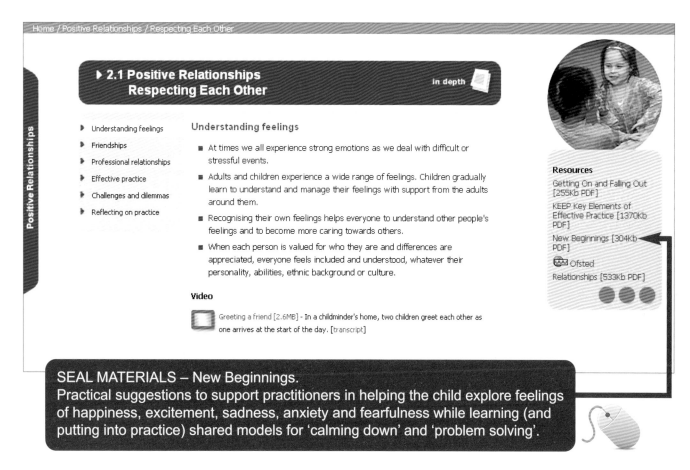

▶ 2.1 Positive Relationships
Respecting Each Other

in depth

- ▶ Understanding feelings
- ▶ Friendships
- ▶ Professional relationships
- ▶ Effective practice
- ▶ Challenges and dilemmas
- ▶ Reflecting on practice

Understanding feelings

- At times we all experience strong emotions as we deal with difficult or stressful events.

- Adults and children experience a wide range of feelings. Children gradually learn to understand and manage their feelings with support from the adults around them.

- Recognising their own feelings helps everyone to understand other people's feelings and to become more caring towards others.

- When each person is valued for who they are and differences are appreciated, everyone feels included and understood, whatever their personality, abilities, ethnic background or culture.

Video

Greeting a friend [2.6MB] - In a childminder's home, two children greet each other as one arrives at the start of the day. [transcript]

Resources

Getting On and Falling Out [255Kb PDF]

KEEP Key Elements of Effective Practice [1370kb PDF]

New Beginnings [304kb PDF]

Ofsted Relationships [533Kb PDF]

SEAL MATERIALS – New Beginnings.
Practical suggestions to support practitioners in helping the child explore feelings of happiness, excitement, sadness, anxiety and fearfulness while learning (and putting into practice) shared models for 'calming down' and 'problem solving'.

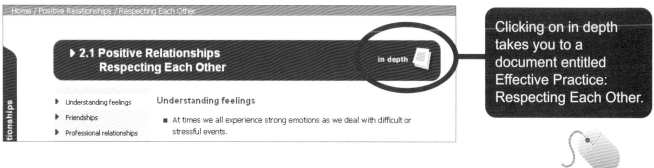

▶ 2.1 Positive Relationships
Respecting Each Other

in depth

- ▶ Understanding feelings
- ▶ Friendships
- ▶ Professional relationships

Understanding feelings

- At times we all experience strong emotions as we deal with difficult or stressful events.

Clicking on in depth takes you to a document entitled Effective Practice: Respecting Each Other.

The document contains the following:

Key messages (summary)

- **Children learn about themselves and others through their relationships with children and adults.**

- **Practitioners need to seek to develop warm, supportive and responsive relationships with children and parents in their care.**

- **Children's social and emotional development is fostered when they feel safe and secure, when they are able to articulate and understand their feelings.**

- **Practitioners need to support children to begin to understand that others may have different needs, feelings and ideas from their own.**

- **Through friendships, children learn to take account of the views of others. This supports their development of interpersonal skills.**

The document gives in-depth information on the following:

What respecting each other means:
- Respect for others is the starting point for the development of good relationships and attachments.
- The importance of developing friendships from an early age.
- That the setting needs to create a climate of mutual respect.

Why respecting each other is important:
- How children become aware of their own special characteristics.
- How children become aware of the needs of others.
- How friendships support children to resolve conflicts.
- How practitioners can respond positively to the dramatic way in which children express their feelings.
- How to develop an effective relationship with parents.

Effective practice in relation to respecting each other:
- Practitioners need to talk about their own feelings when they feel happy or sad.
- Use stories to explore feelings.
- Support children to name and understand feelings.
- Give particular attention to children who appear not to interact with children or adults.
- Model how good relationships can work between practitioners and other professionals who visit the setting.
- Good use of the key person system to support all children but in particular those children with special needs.

Positive Relationships

2.2　Parents as Partners

Action point from Principles into Practice card 2.2

Are there opportunities within the daily routine for informal conversations with parents? Do parents contribute to their child's learning journals?

How to use the CD-ROM to support understanding of 'Parents as Partners'.

Positive Relationships

Children learn to be strong and independent from a base of loving and secure relationships with parents and/or a key person.

▶ **2.1 Respecting Each Other**

▶ **2.2 Parents as Partners**

▶ **2.3 Supporting Learning**

▶ **2.4 Key Person**

Clicking on the commitment Parents as Partners will take you to more information.

▶ **2.2 Positive Relationships**
Parents as Partners

in depth

▶ Respecting diversity
▶ Communication
▶ Learning together
▶ Effective practice
▶ Challenges and dilemmas
▶ Reflecting on practice

Respecting diversity

■ All families are important and should be welcomed and valued in all settings.

■ Families are all different. Children may live with one or both parents, with other relatives or carers, with same sex parents or in an extended family.

■ Families may speak more than one language at home; they may be travellers, refugees or asylum seekers.

■ All practitioners will benefit from professional development in diversity, equality and anti-discriminatory practice whatever the ethnic, cultural or social make-up of the setting.

Video

 Good morning [7MB] - In a childminder's home, the childminder and parent share information as the child settles into the setting. [transcript]

Research

Birth to School Study: A Longitudinal Evaluation of the Peers Early Education Partnership [1259Kb PDF]

 Research Brief: Evaluation of the Special Educational Needs Parent Partnership Services in England

Research Report: Evaluation of the Special Educational Needs Parent Partnership Services in England

Research Brief: Support From the Start

Research Report: Support From the Start

of Parental Involvement, Parental Support and Family Education on Pupil Achievements and Adjustment [178Kb PDF]

 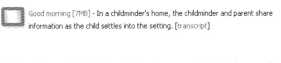 You will need to be connected to the internet to access this detailed report of SEN and parent partnership published in 2006.

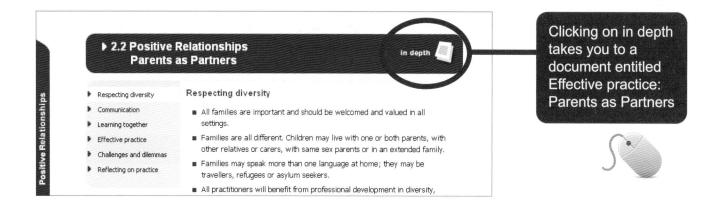

The document contains the following:

Key messages (summary)

- **Parents have the right to be involved in any decisions about their children's care and education.**

- **Children spend a large percentage of their time with their families. When practitioners work in partnership with families it impacts positively on children's well-being and learning.**

- **The importance of developing successful relationships between parents and practitioners.**

The document gives in-depth information on the following:

What Parents as Partners means:
- Recognising the role parents have in giving children confidence and the desire to explore the world
- Sharing and exchanging information with parents about how their child is progressing and the next steps in their learning and development.

Effective practice in relation to parents as partners:
- Recognising that there is not a 'right way' of being a parent. All forms of parenting need to be valued.
- Admission policies may exclude parents simply because they are unable to fill in forms.
- Settings need to ensure they are accessible to the whole community.
- Settings need to consider how they welcome and value all parents but in particular they need to think about how they involve fathers and other significant males. A list of questions supports practitioners to consider how they actively encourage males to feel valued.

Two case studies illustrate the importance of a key person in building relationships with children.

Communication:
- Emphasises the importance of friendly greetings and creating a warm welcoming atmosphere.
- A list of practical suggestions is given to help practitioners effectively communicate with parents and carers.
- Suggestions on how to make letters, brochures and notices more accessible to parents.
- Suggestions are given for involving parents in their child's learning and development and for developing parents' knowledge of how children learn.

Positive Relationships

2.3 Supporting Learning

Do you actively listen to children?

Do you give children thinking time before intervening?

Do you use visual prompts to support children with communication difficulties?

Do you observe children and respond appropriately to encourage and extend curiosity and learning?

How to use the CD-ROM to support understanding of 'Supporting Learning'.

Positive Relationships

Children learn to be strong and independent from a base of loving and secure relationships with parents and/or a key person.

▶ **2.1 Respecting Each Other**

▶ **2.2 Parents as Partners**

▶ **2.3 Supporting Learning**

▶ **2.4 Key Person**

> Clicking on the commitment Supporting Learning will take you to more information

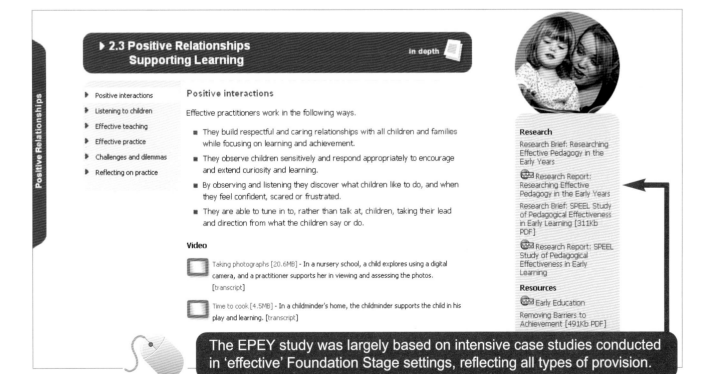

▶ **2.3 Positive Relationships**
Supporting Learning

in depth

- Positive interactions
- Listening to children
- Effective teaching
- Effective practice
- Challenges and dilemmas
- Reflecting on practice

Positive interactions

Effective practitioners work in the following ways.

- They build respectful and caring relationships with all children and families while focusing on learning and achievement.
- They observe children sensitively and respond appropriately to encourage and extend curiosity and learning.
- By observing and listening they discover what children like to do, and when they feel confident, scared or frustrated.
- They are able to tune in to, rather than talk at, children, taking their lead and direction from what the children say or do.

Video

Taking photographs [20.6MB] - In a nursery school, a child explores using a digital camera, and a practitioner supports her in viewing and assessing the photos. [transcript]

Time to cook [4.5MB] - In a childminder's home, the childminder supports the child in his play and learning. [transcript]

Research

Research Brief: Researching Effective Pedagogy in the Early Years

Research Report: Researching Effective Pedagogy in the Early Years

Research Brief: SPEEL Study of Pedagogical Effectiveness in Early Learning [311Kb PDF]

Research Report: SPEEL Study of Pedagogical Effectiveness in Early Learning

Resources

Early Education

Removing Barriers to Achievement [491Kb PDF]

> The EPEY study was largely based on intensive case studies conducted in 'effective' Foundation Stage settings, reflecting all types of provision.

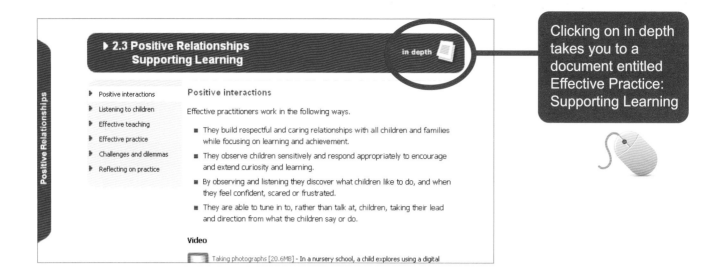

Clicking on in depth takes you to a document entitled Effective Practice: Supporting Learning

The document contains the following:

Key messages (summary)

● **Practitioners need to observe and listen to children and use this information to enable and support children to move to their next steps in learning.**

● **Practitioners need to listen to what parents say about their children and use this information positively to support children in their care.**

● **Practitioners need to provide children with support and reassurance so that they know that they are cared for and valued.**

● **Practitioners need to plan meaningful experiences and activities that take account of children's interests and their stage of development.**

● **Practitioners need to support children's play. Through play children make choices, try out ideas and develop new lines of enquiry.**

The document gives in-depth information on the following:

What supporting learning means:
● People come before equipment.
● Practitioners need to understand how children develop and learn through all the areas of learning and development.
● Understanding the terms 'support' and 'scaffolding'.
● Knowing about individual children, their interests, needs and personal characteristics.
● Observing and assessing children.
● Working in partnership with parents and other professionals.

Why supporting learning is important:
- Children learn best when they feel secure in the knowledge that adults are watching over them.
- Practitioners need to make interaction work by using strategies to support communication.
- Practitioners need to listen to children and be responsive to their needs.
- Practitioners need to listen to parents.
- Practitioners need to create the optimum conditions for learning.
- Practitioners need to observe, enable and facilitate children's learning.

Effective practice in relation to supporting learning:
- Support children's play.
- Provide opportunities for children to develop their speaking, listening and thinking skills.
- Within the daily routine and the learning environment provide opportunities for children to make choices.
- Provide opportunities for EAL children to use their home language.
- Develop a partnership with parents and provide opportunities to listen to and share information.

Listening to children:
- Makes practitioners aware that babies and children who cannot communicate verbally communicate in many other ways.
- Enables practitioners to identify children's needs, interests and stage of development and plan for the next steps in their learning.

Effective teaching:
- Use EYFS to enable children to make progress in their Learning and Development.
- Builds on what children already know and can do.
- Adults provide a running commentary on what children are doing.
- Has clear learning intentions.
- Values children's spontaneous play.
- Takes account of children's interests.

The commitment Supporting Learning has direct links with the commitments: 3.1, 4.1, 4.2, 4.3, 4.4.

2.4 Key Person

Action point from Principles into Practice card 2.4

As part of the induction procedures do you discuss with parents the importance of finding time within their schedules to communicate regularly with their child's key person?
Do you plan time within the daily and weekly routine for each key person to work with parents?

How to use the CD-ROM to support understanding of 'Key Person'

Positive Relationships

Children learn to be strong and independent from a base of loving and secure relationships with parents and/or a key person.

▶ **2.1 Respecting Each Other**

▶ **2.2 Parents as Partners**

▶ **2.3 Supporting Learning**

▶ **2.4 Key Person**

Clicking on the commitment Key Person will take you to more information.

▶ **2.4 Positive Relationships**
Key Person   in depth

▶ Secure attachment
▶ Shared care
▶ Independence
▶ Effective practice
▶ Challenges and dilemmas
▶ Reflecting on practice

Secure attachment

■ A key person helps the baby or child to become familiar with the setting and to feel confident and safe within it.

■ A key person develops a genuine bond with children and offers a settled, close relationship.

■ When children feel happy and secure in this way they are confident to explore and to try out new things.

■ Even when children are older and can hold special people in mind for longer there is still a need for them to have a key person to depend on in the setting, such as their teacher or a teaching assistant.

Research
What Can We Learn from Attachment Research? [138Kb PDF]

Resources
All About...Developing Positive Relations With Children [68Kb PDF]

Attachment and the Key Person Role [16Kb PDF]

 Video

This PDF document by Julian Grenier, head of Kate Greenaway Nursery School, Islington, London, gives examples from practice on how practitioners develop positive relationships with children. She defines the key person approach as being about the commitment to providing consistent care and emotional support to each child, as an individual, throughout the day.

- Secure attachment
- Shared care
- Independence
- Effective practice
- Challenges and dilemmas
- Reflecting on practice

Secure attachment

- A key person helps the baby or child to become familiar with the setting and to feel confident and safe within it.
- A key person develops a genuine bond with children and offers a settled, close relationship.
- When children feel happy and secure in this way they are confident to explore and to try out new things.

Clicking on in depth takes you to a document entitled Effective Practice: Key Person

The document contains the following:

Key messages (summary)

- **Organising the key person approach needs careful planning and development.**

- **Practitioners need to be clear about why the key person commitment is so important.**

- **For the key person approach to be successful, the manager must be commited to the approach.**

- **Practitioners need time to research, develop and deliver the key person approach.**

The document gives in-depth information on the following:

What the key person role means:
- For the baby or young child it means that within the setting there is someone who has special responsibility to support their learning and development and to meet their emotional needs.
- For parents and carers it means they can leave their children confident that within the setting there is someone who loves their baby or child.
- Sharing with parents about their child's day.
- Listening to parents about the pleasures and stresses of bringing up a child.
- For the key person it means professional and emotional commitment.
- For the setting it means that staff provide a higher quality of care and have a greater sense of fulfilment.
- The document examines some concerns that parents may have about the key person approach.

Why the key person is important:
- It supports children to know they are cared for and that someone is looking over them.
- A case study, 'Graham's Story', details how essential the Key Person approach is.

Key person approach in practice:
- Quotes from staff encourage practitioners to reflect upon the following issue – 'How close is too close?'
- Two short scenarios encourage practitioners to reflect upon their practice.
- Emphasises the need for supervision: 'Time to talk and listen individually'.
- Acknowledges that the key person role in reception classes for four and five-year-olds is more difficult. However, where there is more than one adult, teachers need to consider how the teaching assistant can be deployed to support the key person approach.

3 Enabling Environments

Theme: ENABLING ENVIRONMENTS

PRINCIPLE

Every child is a competent learner from birth who can be resilient, capable, confident and self-assured.

The four commitments describe how the principle can be put into practice:

3.1 OBSERVATION, ASSESSMENT AND PLANNING emphasises the need for practitioners to observe children as part of their daily routine. It provides advice on involving parents in the planning and assessment cycle. It stresses the importance of analysing observations to help plan next steps for children. The commitment highlights the importance of recognising that babies and young children are individuals, each with a unique profile of abilities, interests and needs.

3.2 SUPPORTING EVERY CHILD acknowledges that learning is a continuous journey which builds upon each child's past experiences and interests. It provides practitioners with advice on how to use these experiences as a starting point for planning activities that are challenging but achievable. It stresses the importance of supporting children's physical and emotional needs. It emphasises the necessity of parents and professionals working in partnership to support children's learning and progress.

3.3 THE LEARNING ENVIRONMENT provides practitioners with advice on how to create an emotional environment that is secure, warm and welcoming. It states that the indoor and outdoor learning environment has equal status and that practitioners should, wherever possible, provide opportunities for 'free flow' between the indoor and outdoor learning environments. The commitment stresses the importance of providing children with resources that are well maintained, well organised, open ended and appropriate to their stage of development. Children will be confident to investigate, to learn and to make relationships in an environment that is safe and secure.

3.4 THE WIDER CONTEXT acknowledges the importance of working with other agencies, professionals, settings and the local community. In order to achieve the outcomes of *Every Child Matters*, practitioners need to facilitate the effective working across services. They need, for example, to liaise with health visitors, social services and area SENCOs. The commitment stresses the importance of working with the local community, valuing their beliefs, views and backgrounds. It acknowledges the important role practitioners have in supporting the transition process between home and setting, and between setting and setting.

The four Principles into Practice Cards (3.1, 3.2, 3.3 and 3.4), provide practitioners with information about effective practice and give practical suggestions on how to plan an environment that builds on children's interests; how to observe, assess, and plan for the next steps in children's learning; how to support transition and children's progress towards the five outcomes of *Every Child Matters*. They encourage practitioners to reflect upon their practice and identify challenges and dilemmas they may meet in their work with young children.

Enabling Environments

3.1 Observation, Assessment and Planning

Information on this commitment is in chapter 5: Observation, assessment and Planning (see page 47). This is to support practioners in understanding the link between Commitment 3.1 Observation, Assessment and Planning and 4.4 Areas of Learning and Development.

Enabling Environments

3.2 Supporting Every Child

Action point from Principles into Practice card 3.2

How do you as a staff team plan a curriculum that builds on children's individual interests and experiences?

How to use the CD-ROM to implement the commitment 'Supporting Every Child'

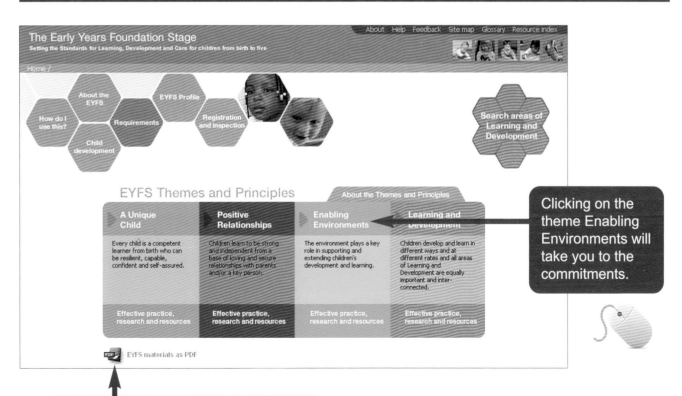

Clicking on the theme Enabling Environments will take you to the commitments.

Clicking on this icon will take you to the EYFS booklets, poster and cards.

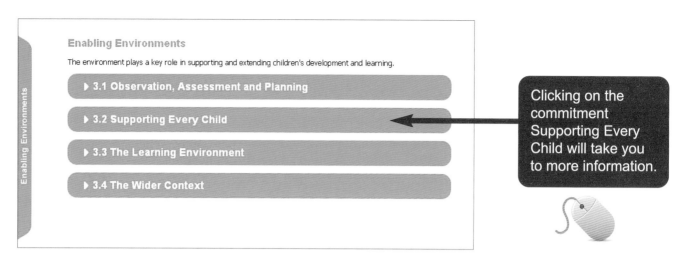

Enabling Environments

The environment plays a key role in supporting and extending children's development and learning.

▶ **3.1 Observation, Assessment and Planning**

▶ **3.2 Supporting Every Child**

▶ **3.3 The Learning Environment**

▶ **3.4 The Wider Context**

Clicking on the commitment Supporting Every Child will take you to more information.

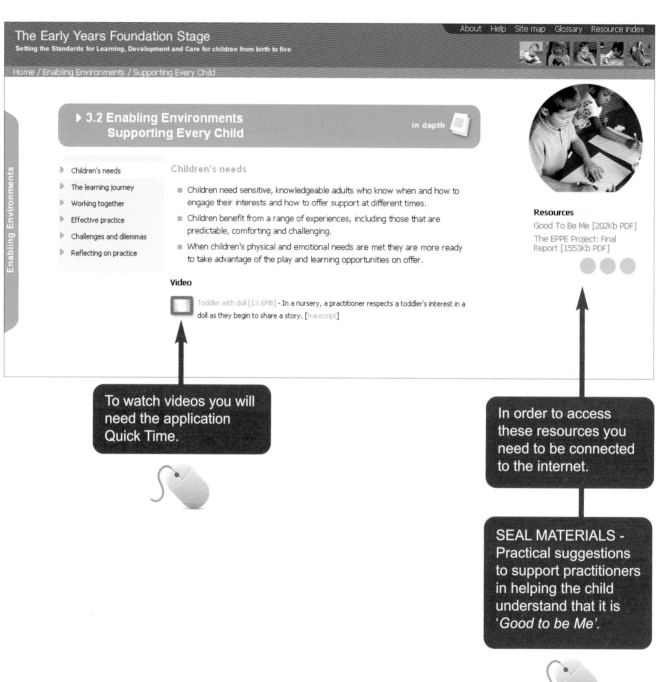

The Early Years Foundation Stage
Setting the Standards for Learning, Development and Care for children from birth to five

About   Help   Site map   Glossary   Resource index

Home / Enabling Environments / Supporting Every Child

▶ **3.2 Enabling Environments**
Supporting Every Child

in depth

- Children's needs
- The learning journey
- Working together
- Effective practice
- Challenges and dilemmas
- Reflecting on practice

Children's needs

- Children need sensitive, knowledgeable adults who know when and how to engage their interests and how to offer support at different times.
- Children benefit from a range of experiences, including those that are predictable, comforting and challenging.
- When children's physical and emotional needs are met they are more ready to take advantage of the play and learning opportunities on offer.

Video

Toddler with doll [13.6MB] - In a nursery, a practitioner respects a toddler's interest in a doll as they begin to share a story. [transcript]

Resources

Good To Be Me [202Kb PDF]
The EPPE Project: Final Report [1553kb PDF]

To watch videos you will need the application Quick Time.

In order to access these resources you need to be connected to the internet.

SEAL MATERIALS - Practical suggestions to support practitioners in helping the child understand that it is *'Good to be Me'*.

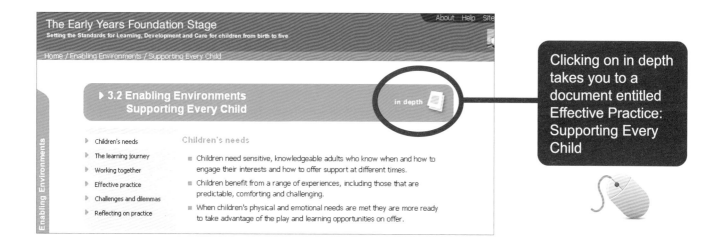

The document contains the following:

Key messages (summary)

- **Identifies the strong influence that the environments in which children grow up have on what they do and can accomplish.**

- **Each child is unique and their needs differ according to their experiences, their cultural and social background.**

- **Practitioners need to create an inclusive environment that meets the identified needs of the children in their care.**

- **Practitioners need to support children to relate new experiences to those experiences that they have already encountered.**

- **Practitioners need to plan for transition. They need to view transition as a process rather than an event and to keep the learning journey smooth at times of transition.**

- **Practitioners need to be proactive in working together with children, families and other professionals. This enables settings to create learning environments that best provide for the needs of all children.**

- **Practitioners should organise the learning environment so that it provides the space and the opportunity for both children and adults to work and play together. This will support the development of positive relationships.**

The document gives in-depth information on the following:

- Why supporting every child is important:

  Children's needs
  - The foundation of enabling learning is to create an environment that is flexible and varied enough to respect and respond to individual needs.
  - In order to learn, they need to be with receptive, knowledgeable, caring adults who understand how to support children's individual learning journeys.

The learning journey

- Most children follow a similar path of development, therefore their learning journeys will be the same in some aspects, but each child may take a different route through that learning journey.
- Practitioners need to create an environment in which the child feels comfortable, but at the same time they need to present enough of the 'new' to stimulate and extend the child.
- This does not mean that all provision must be individualised.

Working together

- Working together with children, families and other professionals will provide children with secure contexts for learning. It will enable practitioners to identify and meet the needs of individual children.
- Children learn from one another, therefore the learning environment and daily routine should actively support children working and playing together.
- Children who experience positive interaction with practitioners form good adult-child relationships.

- **Effective practice in relation to supporting every child:**

Children's needs

- Organising routines and work patterns to meet the needs of the children, not the adults.
- Routines need to have a set pattern so that children know what is happening next.
- Resources need to be organised so that children can access them independently.
- Seek to develop positive relationships with the children's families.
- Use information from other settings, the home or other professionals to plan an environment for learning that will support children to make progress.

The learning journey

- Plan to provide open-ended learning experiences.
- Good storage and retrieval systems enable children to find resources independently.
- Practitioners can support child-initiated learning by adding appropriate resources, modelling, connecting their learning and extending their thinking.
- Ensure that displays and resources reflect children's home communities and the wider world.
- Transition needs to be planned. Children need support to relate their previous experience to their new situation.

Working together

- Observe and talk to children. Use this information when planning the next week's activities. Involving children in the planning process ensures that you are building upon their interests and that what you have planned is meaningful and relevant to children.
- Organise the indoor and outdoor learning environment to support children's interactions with other children.
- Consider ways of developing partnership with parents. Involve parents by sharing observations, encourage parents to contribute to the observation, assessment and record-keeping process.

3.3 The Learning Environment

How do you as a staff team plan a curriculum that builds on children's individual interests and experiences?

How to use the CD-ROM to support understanding of 'The Learning Environment'.

Enabling Environments

The environment plays a key role in supporting and extending children's development and learning.

▶ **3.1 Observation, Assessment and Planning**

▶ **3.2 Supporting Every Child**

▶ **3.3 The Learning Environment**

▶ **3.4 The Wider Context**

Clicking on the commitment The Learning Environment will take you to more information.

▶ **3.3 Enabling Environments**
The Learning Environment

in depth

▶ The emotional environment
▶ The outdoor environment
▶ The indoor environment
▶ Effective practice
▶ Challenges and dilemmas
▶ Reflecting on practice

The outdoor environment

■ Being outdoors has a positive impact on children's sense of well-being and helps all aspects of children's development.

■ Being outdoors offers opportunities for doing things in different ways and on different scales than when indoors.

■ It gives children first-hand contact with weather, seasons and the natural world.

■ Outdoor environments offer children freedom to explore, use their senses, and be physically active and exuberant.

Effective Practice

Outdoor learning [77Kb]

Video

Playing with sand and water [9.3MB] - In the outdoor area on a rainy day at a pre-school, a practitioner explores the effects of water on sand with two children.
[transcript]

Research

Research Brief: Assessing Emotional And Social Competence in Primary School and Early Years Settings

Research Report: Assessing Emotional And Social Competence in Primary School and Early Years Settings

Resources

All of Us - Inclusion Checklist for Settings [1361Kb PDF]

Learning Through Landscapes

Learning through Landscapes: Early Years Vision and Values for Outdoor Play [61Kb PDF]

National Association for Environmental Education

Play England

Safe Early Years

 For more information on The Learning Environment you can click on any research or resource tab.

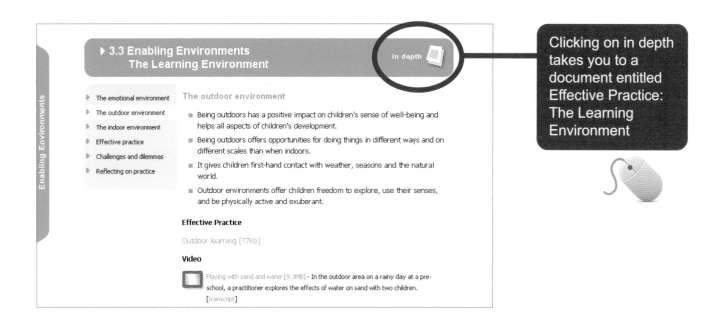

Clicking on in depth takes you to a document entitled Effective Practice: The Learning Environment

The main key message for practitioners is the importance of identifying the need for additional support as early as possible.

The document contains the following:

Key messages (summary)

- **The environment needs to be organised to support active learning.**

- **The environment needs to be organised into areas or zones to provide children with the space to be quiet or noisy, active or still.**

- **When planning the environment, it needs to be appropriate to the age and stage of development of the children.**

- **Health and safety issues, such as security, need to be taken into account.**

- **A range of resources, both natural and manufactured, need to be made available and organised to enable children to access them independently.**

- **A range of activities that support the delivery of the six areas of Learning and Development need to be available.**

- **Ideally, the indoor and outdoor learning environments should be available to children all of the time. This allows children to pursue their own interests and move freely between the indoor and outdoor environment.**

- **The outdoor learning environment needs to offer shade and shelter and a variety of surfaces.**

The document gives in-depth information on the following:

- **Why the learning environment is important:**

  The emotional environment
  - The importance of knowledgeable adults. The document lists what adults should do to support children's learning and development. It stresses the importance of using self-evaluation as a tool to ensure that what is provided is of the highest quality.

  Outdoor and indoor environments
  - It outlines the range and type of resources that should be available for children to experience and explore.
  - It identifies the importance of providing children with challenge and the opportunity to take risks within a safe but interesting environment supported by knowledgeable adults.
  - The need to provide opportunities and time for children to develop gross and fine motor skills, use their senses, develop their imagination, to solve problems, create and design using a range of natural and manufactured materials and resources.

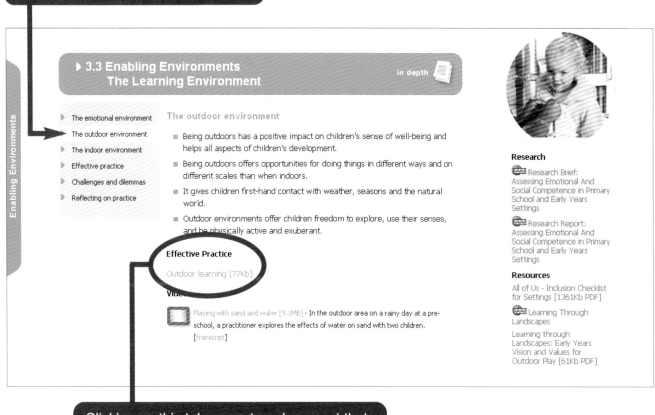

Clicking on The outdoor environment in the grey panel to the left of the screen takes you to more information about the outdoor environment

▶ 3.3 Enabling Environments
The Learning Environment
in depth

Enabling Environments

- The emotional environment
- The outdoor environment
- The indoor environment
- Effective practice
- Challenges and dilemmas
- Reflecting on practice

The outdoor environment

- Being outdoors has a positive impact on children's sense of well-being and helps all aspects of children's development.
- Being outdoors offers opportunities for doing things in different ways and on different scales than when indoors.
- It gives children first-hand contact with weather, seasons and the natural world.
- Outdoor environments offer children freedom to explore, use their senses, and be physically active and exuberant.

Effective Practice

Outdoor learning [77Kb]

Video

Playing with sand and water [9.3MB] - In the outdoor area on a rainy day at a pre-school, a practitioner explores the effects of water on sand with two children.
[transcript]

Research

Research Brief: Assessing Emotional And Social Competence in Primary School and Early Years Settings

Research Report: Assessing Emotional And Social Competence in Primary School and Early Years Settings

Resources

All of Us - Inclusion Checklist for Settings [1361Kb PDF]

Learning Through Landscapes

Learning through Landscapes: Early Years Vision and Values for Outdoor Play [61Kb PDF]

Clicking on this takes you to a document that gives detailed practical advice on developing the outdoor learning environment.

Enabling Environments

3.4   The Wider Context

Action point from Principles into Practice card 3.4

When children in your care attend several settings, how do you ensure that you regularly share the children's development and learning records and any other relevant information?

How to use the CD-ROM to support understanding of 'The Wider Context'

Enabling Environments

The environment plays a key role in supporting and extending children's development and learning.

▸ **3.1 Observation, Assessment and Planning**

▸ **3.2 Supporting Every Child**

▸ **3.3 The Learning Environment**

▸ **3.4 The Wider Context**

Clicking on the commitment The Wider Context will take you to more information.

▸ **3.4 Enabling Environments**
The Wider Context   in depth

- Transitions and continuity
- Multi-agency working
- The community
- Effective practice
- Challenges and dilemmas
- Reflecting on practice

Transitions and continuity

- Children may move between several different settings in the course of a day, a week, a month or a year.
- Children's social, emotional and educational needs are central to any transition between one setting and another or within one setting.
- Some children and their parents will find transition times stressful while others will enjoy the experience.
- Effective communication between settings is key to ensuring that children's needs are met and there is continuity in their learning.

Research

 Early Years Transition and Special Educational Needs

Research Brief: An Exploration of Different Models of Multi-Agency Partnerships in Key Worker Services for Disabled Children [309Kb PDF]

Research Report: An Exploration of Different Models of Multi-Agency Partnerships in Key Worker Services for Disabled Children

Research Brief: Developing Information Sharing and Assessment Systems [377Kb PDF]

Research Report: Developing Information Sharing and Assessment Systems

Research Brief: Early Years Transitions and Special Educational Needs [514Kb PDF]

Video

 A visit from the Community Support Officer [5.8MB] - A Community Support Officer visits a local nursery, and talks with the children in the outdoor play area about his uniform and walkie talkie [transcript]

For more information on The Wider Context, you can click on any research or resources tab.

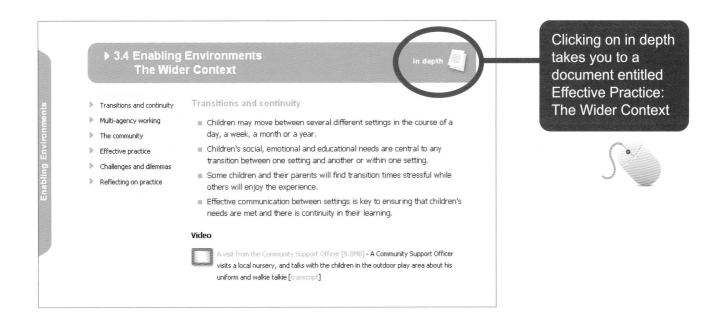

Clicking on in depth takes you to a document entitled Effective Practice: The Wider Context

The document contains the following:

Key messages (summary)

- Partnerships between providers and other agencies in the local community enhance practice and create consistency and quality in the care and education of all children.

- Effective communication between families, practitioners, settings and other agencies is vital. It ensures that children's needs, interests and next steps in their stage of development are shared. When children are settled and cared for, they thrive and develop a positive disposition for learning.

- Children need to be prepared for change. Any times of transition should be seen as a process not a one-off event.

The document gives in-depth information on the following:

What the wider context means:

- Practitioners need to positively plan to support those children who attend more than one setting in a day. They need to develop strategies to enable children to link their learning and feel secure.
- Through effective liaison with other settings, transition needs to be managed well.

Effective practice in relation to the wider context:

Transitions and continuity

- Children will need different levels of support when moving from setting to setting. Practitioners should use their knowledge of the child to identify the level and the type of support the child needs.
- When a child attends two settings on the same day, the child's key person in each setting should liaise and plan together by sharing information about the child's interests and the stage they have reached in their learning and development.

- Children should be encouraged to welcome new children into their setting.
- Wherever possible, practitioners should arrange a home visit before the child is admitted to the setting.
- Involve parents in the transition process: before, during and after the move to the new setting.
- In order for successful transition to take place, practitioners working in Year 1 need to have a working knowledge of the EYFS and the EYFS profile (EYFSP).
- Schools should analyse EYFSP and Communication, Language and Literacy Development (CLLD) assessment data, gathered on transition from reception to Year 1, to identify strengths and points for development in provision for the EYFS. Such analyses should provide comparisons of achievement for different groups, for example, by gender, ethnicity or where English is an additional language.

Multi-agency working
- Identifies good practice when supporting a child with special needs.
- Having a policy for transition, continuity and interagency working that is shared with all those who are involved in the child's life supports the development of good practice.

The community
- Practical suggestions are given for involving the local community and community groups in the setting.
- Staff need to know about the culture and the distinctive nature of the community in which they work. This knowledge can be used to support children's learning and development.

4 Learning and Development

Theme: LEARNING AND DEVELOPMENT

> **PRINCIPLE**
> Children develop and learn in different ways and at different rates and all areas of Learning and Development are equally important and inter-connected.

The four commitments describe how the principle can be put into practice:

4.1 PLAY AND EXPLORATION acknowledges that the highest level of learning takes place during play. It is through play that children try out ideas, re-live experiences and learn new concepts and skills. It provides practitioners with advice on how to support and extend children's play. The commitment emphasises that children need space and open-ended resources. Practitioners need to value children's play, which develops naturally and spontaneously.

4.2 ACTIVE LEARNING acknowledges that children need mental and physical challenges. They learn best when they have the opportunity to use their senses to investigate objects and materials. The commitment emphasises that when children become actively involved in finding out about the world around them they feel a sense of achievement. This has a positive impact on their emotional well-being. It provides practitioners with advice on how to support, extend and personalise each child's learning journey.

4.3 CREATIVITY AND CRITICAL THINKING acknowledges that being creative involves all areas of learning – it is not necessarily about making an end product. The learning environment needs to be organised to allow children to make connections in their learning. The commitment stresses the importance of practitioners and children working together to develop an idea or skill. It provides practitioners with advice on how to record the learning that has taken place, how to get involved in the thinking process and how to use children's interest as a vehicle for learning.

4.4 AREAS OF LEARNING AND DEVELOPMENT states that the EYFS is made up of six areas of Learning and Development. It acknowledges all areas of Learning and Development are connected to one another and are equally important. The commitment stresses that all areas of Learning and Development are underpinned by the Principles of the EYFS. Each area of Learning and Development is further divided into aspects (there are 28 in total. Each area of Learning and Development card provides practitioners with advice on how to implement that particular area and gives examples of effective practice).

The four Principles into Practice cards 4.1, 4.2, 4.3 and 4.4, and the six Learning and Development cards provide practitioners with information about effective practice and give practical suggestions on how to develop positive relationships, to create enabling environments and support children's Learning and Development. They encourage practitioners to reflect upon their practice and identify challenges and dilemmas they may meet in their work with young children and their families.

Learning and Development

4.1 Play and Exploration

Action point from Principles into Practice card 4.1

Do you provide flexible resources that can be used in many different ways?
Do you support children's role play by story telling and providing the appropriate props?

How to use the CD-ROM to implement the commitment 'Play and Exploration'.

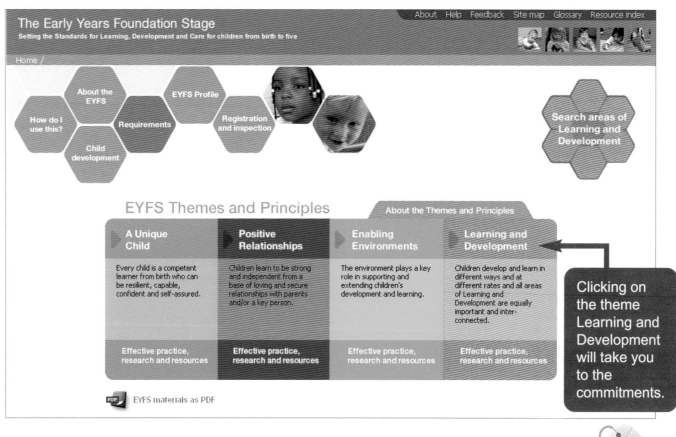

The Early Years Foundation Stage
Setting the Standards for Learning, Development and Care for children from birth to five

About   Help   Feedback   Site map   Glossary   Resource index

Home /

About the EYFS

How do I use this?

Requirements

Child development

EYFS Profile

Registration and inspection

Search areas of Learning and Development

EYFS Themes and Principles

About the Themes and Principles

A Unique Child	Positive Relationships	Enabling Environments	Learning and Development
Every child is a competent learner from birth who can be resilient, capable, confident and self-assured.	Children learn to be strong and independent from a base of loving and secure relationships with parents and/or a key person.	The environment plays a key role in supporting and extending children's development and learning.	Children develop and learn in different ways and at different rates and all areas of Learning and Development are equally important and inter-connected.
Effective practice, research and resources	Effective practice, research and resources	Effective practice, research and resources	Effective practice, research and resources

EYFS materials as PDF

Clicking on the theme Learning and Development will take you to the commitments.

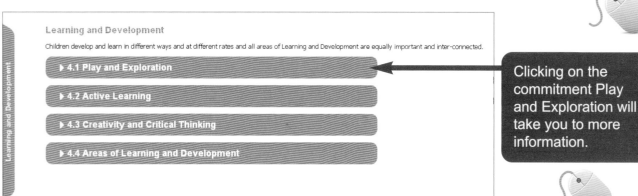

Learning and Development

Children develop and learn in different ways and at different rates and all areas of Learning and Development are equally important and inter-connected.

▶ 4.1 Play and Exploration

▶ 4.2 Active Learning

▶ 4.3 Creativity and Critical Thinking

▶ 4.4 Areas of Learning and Development

Clicking on the commitment Play and Exploration will take you to more information.

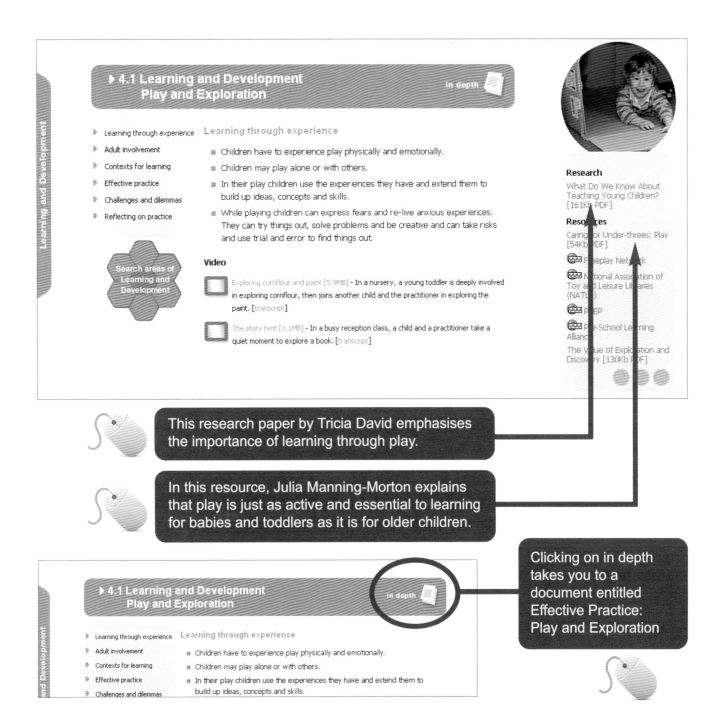

This research paper by Tricia David emphasises the importance of learning through play.

In this resource, Julia Manning-Morton explains that play is just as active and essential to learning for babies and toddlers as it is for older children.

Clicking on in depth takes you to a document entitled Effective Practice: Play and Exploration

The document contains the following:

Key messages (summary)

- Play and exploration promotes brain development.

- Play involves a child playing alone, alongside another child or co-operatively with another child, children and or an adult.

- During play, children's concepts, skills, attitudes and achievements are extended.

- Practitioners provide children with space, open-ended resources and time.

- Practitioners provide the appropriate level of support.

- Practitioners create an enabling environment.

The document gives in-depth information on the following:

What play and exploration means:
- Children are able to choose from a range of adult-directed and child-initiated activities.
- Practitioners need to observe children's interests, learning styles and stages of development.
- Children can play alone or with others.
- The definition of play is explored.
- Free-flow play is discussed.

Why play and exploration is important:
- A comprehensive list is given of the opportunities that play and exploration provide.

Effective practice in relation to play and exploration:
- Learning through first-hand experiences, not by means of a worksheet.
- Provision of appropriate, inexpensive resources.
- Resources need to be well organised and accessible.
- Practitioners need to build on children's familiar experiences.
- Children concentrate for extended periods of time in self-chosen tasks.

Adult involvement:
- Practitioners need to plan and resource a challenging environment where they can support and extend children's play.
- Practitioners need to be aware that it is sometimes important not to interrupt when children are deeply involved in their learning through play.
- Practitioners need to develop their skills of observation so that they know what a child can do and what they are trying to achieve next.

Effective Provision of Pre-school Education Project (EPPE) (Sylva et al., 2003) has now confirmed the centrality of play in early learning. (The EPPE research can be found under the Theme Enabling Environments, commitment 3.2 Supporting Every Child.)

Contexts for learning:
- Children do not separate their experiences into play and learning since they learn as they play and can have fun while they learn. There are therefore many contexts for children's learning.

Dispositions for learning:
- Researchers identify involvement and well-being as central processes in learning.
- The type of learners children become will be influenced by their environment.
- Practitioners need to provide children with challenging activities that invite involvement. This will enable children to make choices.

Learning and Development

4.2 Active Learning

Action point from Principles into Practice card 4.2

How do you as a staff team plan a curriculum that builds on children's individual interests and experiences?

How to use the CD-ROM to support understanding of 'Active Learning'.

Learning and Development

Children develop and learn in different ways and at different rates and all areas of Learning and Development are equally important and inter-connected.

▶ **4.1 Play and Exploration**

▶ **4.2 Active Learning**

▶ **4.3 Creativity and Critical Thinking**

▶ **4.4 Areas of Learning and Development**

Clicking on the commitment Active Learning will take you to more information.

▶ 4.2 Learning and Development Active Learning

in depth

▶ Mental and physical involvement

▶ Decision making

▶ Personalised learning

▶ Effective practice

▶ Challenges and dilemmas

▶ Reflecting on practice

Search areas of Learning and Development

Mental and physical involvement

- To be mentally or physically engaged in learning, children need to feel at ease, secure and confident.

- Active learning occurs when children are keen to learn and are interested in finding things out for themselves.

- When children are actively involved in learning they gain a sense of satisfaction from their explorations and investigations.

- When children engage with people, materials, objects, ideas or events they test things out and solve problems. They need adults to challenge and extend their thinking.

Video

Block play [6.5MB] - In a nursery school, a small group of children work together on a large construction, and afterwards their work-in-progress is cordoned off, showing that their achievement is respected. [transcript]

Research

Research Brief: The Effects of the Peers Early Educational Partnership (PEEP) on Children's Developmental Progress

Research Report: The Effects of the Peers Early Educational Partnership (PEEP) on Children's Developmental Progress

Resources

Going for Goals! [189Kb PDF]

Starting Strong, Curricula and Pedagogies in Early Childhood Education and Care [170Kb PDF]

This resource provides information on five curriculum outlines:

- Experiential Education
- The High/Scope® Curriculum
- The Reggio Emilia Approach
- Te Whāriki
- The Swedish curriculum

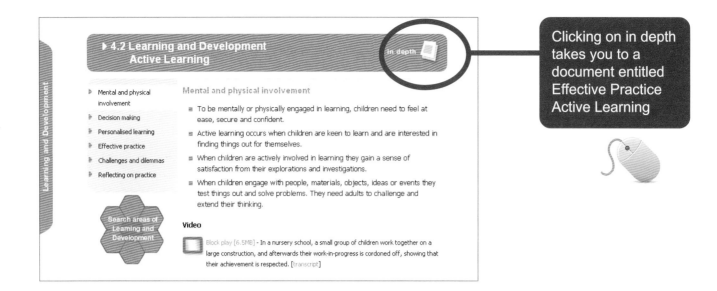

The document contains the following:

Key messages (summary)

- **Children learn by actively investigating the world around them.**

- **Practitioners need to create an environment that supports children's involvement in active learning.**

- **Children need to be encouraged to make decisions about their learning.**

- **The range of activities available should take account of children's interests and stage of development.**

The document gives in-depth information on the following:

What active learning means:
- As children investigate their world, they not only physically investigate but they begin to construct ideas about the world around them and try to make sense of their experiences. Active learning enables them to develop as learners.

Why active learning is important:
- Action, both physical and mental, enables children to make sense of the world.
- Their interactions with people and things are central to the learning process.
- Children need to be in a physical and emotional environment that promotes children's active involvement.
- Describes what 'active learning' looks like in practice.

Decision-making:

- Children need a learning environment that is stimulating and well organised, where learning is matched to their interests. In this environment children can make decisions about their learning.
- Children need to be allowed to make decisions about what and how they are going to do things.
- Practitioners need to create situations where children need to make decisions.
- Practitioners need to actively support the decisions children make.

Personalised learning:

- Importance of valuing children as individuals enables practitioners to make learning meaningful for each child.
- Building relationships with children and parents will help practitioners to understand what interests individual children.
- Practitioners need to plan a range of activities that cater for all learning styles, stages of development and interests.
- Practitioners need to consider the context of the activities that are presented to children. They will only be motivated to take part in an activity if they find some meaning in it.

Effective practice in relation to active learning:

- Plan play that is based on children's first-hand experiences.
- Ensure that the daily routine is flexible.
- Use visual and auditory prompts.
- Use materials that children can explore through their senses.
- Make full use of the outdoor classroom.
- Support children's play.

Decision-making:

- Good storage and retrieval systems enable children to make choices.
- To extend children's learning, plan activities that relate to their choice.
- Observing children will provide information on what activities a child chooses to do and what activities they avoid. This information should be used to deepen their learning and widen their interest.

Personalised learning:

- Use information gathered from parents and from the observation and assessment process to provide activities that build on what children already know.
- Provide appropriate support for children with special needs and those with English as an additional language (commitment 1.2).
- Provide opportunities for EAL children to use their home language within the setting.
- Monitor children's progress against the development matters guidance. If areas of concern arise, seek appropriate support from within the setting or from other agencies.

4.3 Creativity and Critical Thinking

Action point from Principles into Practice card 4.3

Are there good storage and retrieval systems in place which allow children to have independent access to a range of materials and resources?
Do children have the freedom to design and make their own cards, for example, for Christmas, Mother's Day?

How to use the CD-ROM to support understanding of 'Creativity and Critical Thinking'

Learning and Development

Children develop and learn in different ways and at different rates and all areas of Learning and Development are equally important and inter-connected.

▶ **4.1 Play and Exploration**

▶ **4.2 Active Learning**

▶ **4.3 Creativity and Critical Thinking**

▶ **4.4 Areas of Learning and Development**

Clicking on the commitment Creating and Critical Thinking will take you to more information

▶ **4.3 Learning and Development**
Creativity and Critical Thinking
in depth

▶ Making connections
▶ Transforming understanding
▶ Sustained shared thinking
▶ Effective practice
▶ Challenges and dilemmas
▶ Reflecting on practice

Making connections

■ Being creative involves the whole curriculum, not just the arts. It is not necessarily about making an end-product such as a picture, song or play.

■ Children will more easily make connections between things they've learned if the environment encourages them to do so. For example, they need to be able to fetch materials easily and to be able to move them from one place to another.

■ Effective practitioners value each child's culture and help them to make connections between experiences at home, the setting and the wider community.

■ It is difficult for children to make creative connections in learning when colouring in a worksheet or making a Diwali card just like everyone else's.

Search areas of Learning and Development

Video

 Pirates' treasure [28.1MB] - In a pre-school, a practitioner offers resources, questions and ideas to a child exploring 'pirates'. [transcript]

Research

Research Brief: Researching Effective Pedagogy in the Early Years [378Kb PDF]

Research Report: Researching Effective Pedagogy in the Early Years

Resources

Government Response to Paul Roberts' Report on Nurturing Creativity in Young People [159Kb PDF]

Messy Play [72Kb PDF]

Overview: Nurturing Creativity in Young People [961Kb PDF]

Nurturing Creativity in Young People

Messy Play is a document written by Bernadette Duffy. 'Despite appearances, messy play can make an enormous contribution to babies' and young children's cognitive and creative development.' The document outlines how messy play can support all six areas of Learning and Development.

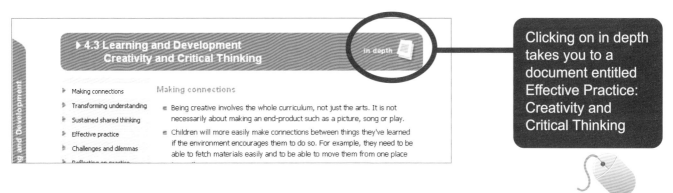

Clicking on in depth takes you to a document entitled Effective Practice: Creativity and Critical Thinking

The document contains the following:

Key messages (summary)

- **Creativity emerges when children have the freedom and time to explore the world around them.**

- **Creativity can be supported by sensitive practitioners who listen to children and follow their lead.**

- **Creativity and critical thinking can be fostered when practitioners use their knowledge to support children to make new connections and new meaning.**

- **Creativity fosters critical thinking by allowing children to review and reinvent.**

The document gives in-depth information on the following:

What creativity and critical thinking means:

- Making connections between things, people or places in ways that are new and personally meaningful. They occur in all areas of Learning and Development.

Why creativity and critical thinking is important:

- Creativity often does not have an end product – it is a process.
- This creative process enables new learning to take place.
- When children are involved in exploring and investigating places and things, creativity emerges.
- Practitioners need to be tuned into and be attentive to a child's exploration. Their presence empowers children to experiment and take risks.

Effective practice in relation to creativity and critical thinking:

- Make connections between planned adult-led activities and adult-directed activities within the continuous provision.
- Ensure that all children have access to materials, resources and situations.
- Provide stimuli such as stories to stimulate children's imagination.
- Use information about children's interests as a context for stimulating creativity.
- Create an environment where children can express their ideas through a range of media.
- Organise resources and materials so they are accessible to all children.
- Give children the freedom to move materials and resources from one area to another.
- Consider how you can promote creativity by creating hidden areas within the environment and by adding or changing resources.
- Give children time to create, explore and develop their initiatives.
- Give children time to think and reflect upon their learning.
- Sensitively support children's ideas by listening to their suggestions. Extend their thinking further by posing questions and suggesting alternative solutions.

Learning and Development

Children develop and learn in different ways and at different rates and all areas of Learning and Development are equally important and inter-connected.

▸ 4.1 Play and Exploration

▸ 4.2 Active Learning

▸ 4.3 Creativity and Critical Thinking

▸ 4.4 Areas of Learning and Development

Clicking on the commitment Areas of Learning and Development will take you to more information

---

▸ 4.4 Learning and Development
Areas of Learning and Development

- Introduction
- Personal, Social and Emotional Development
- Communication, Language and Literacy
- Problem Solving, Reasoning and Numeracy
- Knowledge and Understanding of the World
- Physical Development
- Creative Development
- Resources: Early Reading

Search areas of Learning and Development

Introduction

The EYFS is made up of six areas of Learning and Development. All areas of Learning and Development are connected to one another and are equally important. All areas of Learning and Development are underpinned by the principles of the EYFS.

The areas of Learning and Development are:

- Personal, Social and Emotional Development
- Communication, Language and Literacy
- Problem Solving, Reasoning and Numeracy
- Knowledge and Understanding of the World
- Physical Development
- Creative Development.

Learning and Development

- The six areas of Learning and Development together make up the skills, knowledge and experiences appropriate for babies and children as they grow, learn and develop.
- Although these are presented as separate areas, it is important to remember that for children everything links and nothing is compartmentalised.
- The challenge for practitioners is to ensure that children's learning and development occur as an outcome of their individual interests and abilities

Video

There are video clips under each area of Learning and Development

Research

Independent Review of the Teaching of Early Reading [431Kb PDF]

Research Brief: A Systematic Review of the Research Literature on the Use of Phonics in the Teaching of Reading and Spelling [206Kb PDF]

www Research Report: A Systematic Review of the Research Literature on the Use of Phonics in the Teaching of Reading and Spelling

Resources

www Association for Physical Education

Booktouch [1143Kb PDF]

www Department for Children, Schools and Families

Clicking on the flower will enable you to refine your search within the areas of Learning and Development.

Detailed information on using this tool is in **Chapter 5** (see page 56).

> ▶ 4.4 Learning and Development
> Areas of Learning and Development

Clicking on an area of Learning and Development provides practitioners with detailed information about the content of each aspect and what this means for practice.

Search areas of Learning and Development

Problem Solving, Reasoning and Numeracy

Requirements

Children must be supported in developing their understanding of Problem Solving, Reasoning and Numeracy in a broad range of contexts in which they can explore, enjoy, learn, practise and talk about their developing understanding. They must be provided with opportunities to practise and extend their skills in these areas and to gain confidence and competence in their use.

Aspects of Problem Solving, Reasoning and Numeracy

Problem Solving, Reasoning and Numeracy is made up of the following aspects:

Numbers as Labels and for Counting - is about how children gradually know and use numbers and counting in play, and eventually recognise and use numbers reliably, to develop mathematical ideas and to solve problems.

Calculating - is about how children develop an awareness of the relationship between numbers and amounts and know that numbers can be combined to be 'added together' and can be separated by 'taking away' and that two or more amounts can be compared.

Shape, Space and Measures - is about how through talking about shapes and quantities, and developing appropriate vocabulary, children use their knowledge to develop ideas and to solve mathematical problems.

Video

Getting ready to go out [6.2MB] - In a reception class, the practitioner encourages children to locate their wellingtons by number and location. [transcript]

A picture of my family [6.8MB] - In a pre-school, a practitioner supports two children to think about biggest, smallest, tallest and shortest, as they discuss the pictures they have drawn. [transcript]

Cocoa for 50p [6.2MB] - In the outdoor area of a pre-school on a sunny day, the practitioner supports a child in his role-play about shops and money. [transcript]

Talking about a monster [9.1MB] - In a reception class, the practitioner supports a child to talk about the features of his 'monster' using language such as long, tall, taller. [transcript]

A bed for a giant [19.2MB] - In a reception class, the practitioner supports a child to solve problems by thinking about the size of a giant's bed, and helping him learn new skills about measuring. [transcript]

To watch videos you will need the application Quick Time.

5 Observation, Assessment and Planning

Commitments 3.1 and 4.4 are covered here together as a separate chapter because practitioners need to use both commitments together if they are to provide an effective curriculum that builds upon the child's interest and meets their individual needs. Once practitioners have observed what the child can do, they need to use the Development matters, Look, listen and note, Effective practice and planning and resourcing section of the commitment 4.4 Areas of Learning and Development to plan the next steps in the child's learning. These two commitments are completely intertwined and dependent on each other. Practitioners need to view these two commitments as one.

Where do I find out about observation, assessment and planning?

Theme: ENABLING ENVIRONMENTS

In the commitment
3.1 OBSERVATION, ASSESSMENT AND PLANNING

This commitment provides practitioners with information to support the observation, assessment and planning process.

The principle for this theme emphasises the environment (indoor, outdoor and emotional) and the key role this plays in supporting observation, assessment and planning.

Principles into Practice card 3.1 provides practitioners with information about effective practice. The card emphasises the need to observe children to find out about what they can do, their interests and needs.

Action point from card 3.1

Plan to observe as part of your daily routine.

How to use the CD-ROM to support the 'Observation, Assessment and Planning Process'.

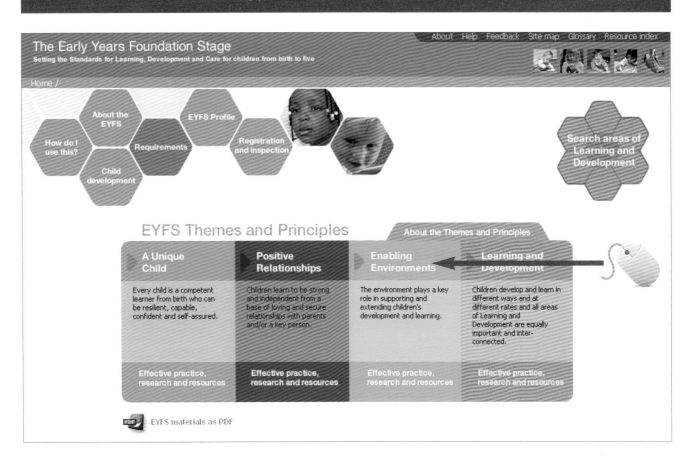

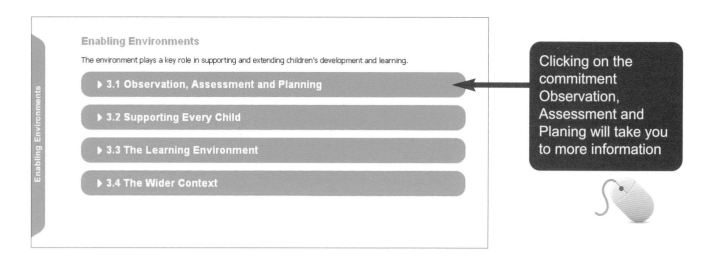

Enabling Environments

The environment plays a key role in supporting and extending children's development and learning.

▸ 3.1 Observation, Assessment and Planning

▸ 3.2 Supporting Every Child

▸ 3.3 The Learning Environment

▸ 3.4 The Wider Context

Clicking on the commitment Observation, Assessment and Planing will take you to more information

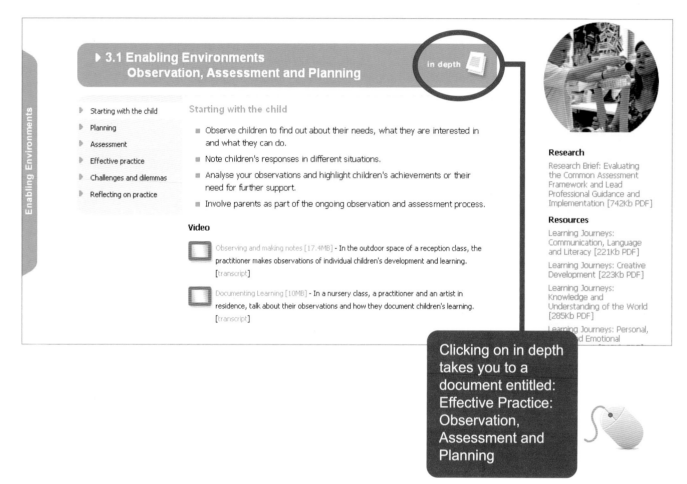

▸ 3.1 Enabling Environments
Observation, Assessment and Planning

in depth

- Starting with the child
- Planning
- Assessment
- Effective practice
- Challenges and dilemmas
- Reflecting on practice

Starting with the child

- Observe children to find out about their needs, what they are interested in and what they can do.
- Note children's responses in different situations.
- Analyse your observations and highlight children's achievements or their need for further support.
- Involve parents as part of the ongoing observation and assessment process.

Video

Observing and making notes [17.4MB] - In the outdoor space of a reception class, the practitioner makes observations of individual children's development and learning. [transcript]

Documenting Learning [10MB] - In a nursery class, a practitioner and an artist in residence, talk about their observations and how they document children's learning. [transcript]

Research

Research Brief: Evaluating the Common Assessment Framework and Lead Professional Guidance and Implementation [742Kb PDF]

Resources

Learning Journeys: Communication, Language and Literacy [221Kb PDF]

Learning Journeys: Creative Development [223Kb PDF]

Learning Journeys: Knowledge and Understanding of the World [285Kb PDF]

Learning Journeys: Personal, ...d Emotional

Clicking on in depth takes you to a document entitled: Effective Practice: Observation, Assessment and Planning

The document contains the following:

Key messages (summary)

- **Observation, assessment and planning all support children's development and learning. Planning starts with observing children in order to understand and consider their current interests, development and learning.**

OBSERVATION
Observation describes the process of watching the children in our care, listening to them and taking note of what we see and hear.

We assess children's progress by analysing our observations and deciding what they tell us. We also need to find out about children's care and learning needs from their parents. From these we can identify the children's requirements, interests, current development and learning.

We plan for the next steps in children's development and learning. Much of this needs to be done on the basis of what we have found out from our own observations and assessments as well as information from parents.

The document gives in-depth information on the following topics:

- Observation skills
- Types of observation
- Recording observations
- Involving children in the assessment process
- Involving parents in the assessment process
- Assessment for learning
- Formative assessment
- Summative assessment
- The Common Assessment Framework (CAF)

The diagram below, taken from the document 'Effective Practice: Observation, Assessment and Planning' (page 5), shows how Observation, Assessment and Planning all feed into one another and contribute to our knowledge about the child.

Planning
What next?
Experiences and opportunities, learning environment, resources, routines, practitioner's role.

The child

Start Here
Observation
Look, listen and note.
Describing

Assessment
Analysing observations and **deciding** what they tell us about children.

Further information on involving parents in the assessment process can be found in the in depth section of Parents as partners – commitment 2.2.

Planning

The document identifies three levels of planning:

- **Long-term planning;**
- **Medium-term planning;**
- **Short-term planning.**

There is a detailed explanation of each type of planning in the document.

The Planning and resourcing section of the *Practice Guidance* states: 'Good planning is the key to making children's learning effective, exciting, varied and progressive.' It goes on, 'The process works best when all practitioners working in the setting are involved'. *(Practice Guidance page 12, 2.8)*

Planning together provides opportunities to share knowledge about how individual children learn and make progress. It enables practitioners to consider how the organisation and resourcing of the learning environment effectively supports the delivery of the planned curriculum.

Does the learning environment provide opportunities for independent learning and sustained shared thinking?

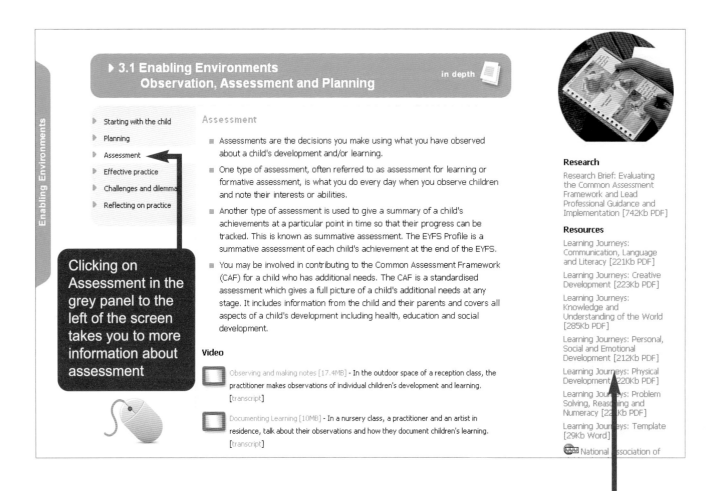

▶ **3.1 Enabling Environments**
Observation, Assessment and Planning

Planning

- Planning can be for the long-/medium-term and can show how the Principles of the EYFS will be put into practice.

- Some planning will be short-term – for a week or a day and will show how you will support each child's learning and development.

- This planning always follows the same pattern – observe, analyse, and use what you have found out about the children in your group so that you plan for the next steps in their learning.

Clicking on Planning in the grey panel to the left of the screen takes you to more information about planning

Video

 Observing and making notes [17.4MB] - In the outdoor space of a reception class, the practitioner makes observations of individual children's development and learning. [transcript]

 Documenting Learning [10MB] - In a nursery class, a practitioner and an artist in residence, talk about their observations and how they document children's learning. [transcript]

Examples of planning ➡

Nursery Planning: Planning For 2-Year Olds [101Kb PDF]

Nursery Planning: Planning For 3 and 4-Year Olds [235Kb PDF]

Nursery Planning: Planning For 3 to 4-Year Olds [181Kb PDF]

Planning From Birth [187Kb PDF]

Reception Class [80Kb PDF]

How do I know what to observe, assess and plan?

THEME: Learning and Development

In the commitment
4.4 Areas of Learning and Development

This commitment identifies the skills, knowledge and experiences appropriate for children from birth to five. The Learning and Development section is split into four sections:

- Development matters
- Look listen and note
- Effective practice
- Planning and resourcing.

The flower icon tool on the CD-ROM enables you to view these sections for each area of Learning and Development. Detailed instructions on how to use this facility can be found on page 56.

The principle for this theme emphasises that children will not necessarily progress sequentially through all the stages of development.

> **LEARNING AND DEVELOPMENT PRINCIPLE**
> Children develop and learn in different ways and at different rates and all areas of Learning and Development are equally important and inter-connected.

Principles into Practice card 4.4 states that:

'There are separate requirements for each area of Learning and Development shown in 'Requirements' on each of the areas of Learning and Development cards. The requirements set out what practitioners must provide in order to support babies' and children's development and learning in each aspect and area of Learning and Development of the EYFS.'

These requirements can be found on the following pages of the *Practice Guidance* revised edition May 2008.

Area of Learning and Development	Practice Guidance
Personal, Social and Emotional Development	Page 24
Communication Language and Literacy	Page 41
Problem Solving, Reasoning and Numeracy	Page 63
Knowledge and Understanding of the World	Page 77
Physical Development	Page 92
Creative Development	Page 106

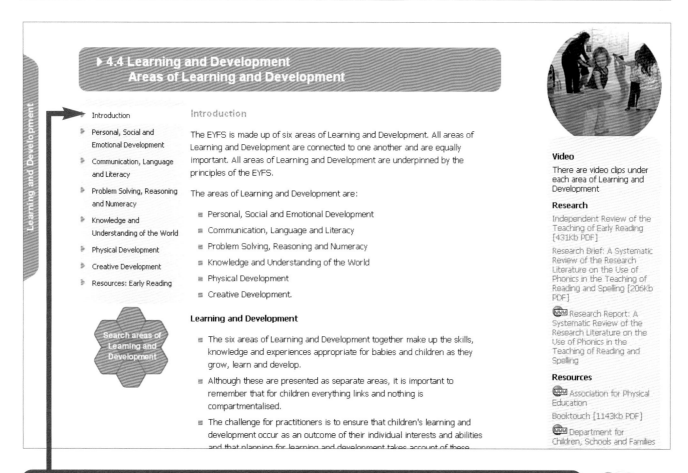

Learning and Development

Children develop and learn in different ways and at different rates and all areas of Learning and Development are equally important and inter-connected.

▶ 4.1 Play and Exploration

▶ 4.2 Active Learning

▶ 4.3 Creativity and Critical Thinking

▶ 4.4 Areas of Learning and Development

Search areas of Learning and Development

▶ 4.4 Learning and Development
Areas of Learning and Development

Introduction
Personal, Social and Emotional Development
Communication, Language and Literacy
Problem Solving, Reasoning and Numeracy
Knowledge and Understanding of the World
Physical Development
Creative Development
Resources: Early Reading

Search areas of Learning and Development

Introduction

The EYFS is made up of six areas of Learning and Development. All areas of Learning and Development are connected to one another and are equally important. All areas of Learning and Development are underpinned by the principles of the EYFS.

The areas of Learning and Development are:

- Personal, Social and Emotional Development
- Communication, Language and Literacy
- Problem Solving, Reasoning and Numeracy
- Knowledge and Understanding of the World
- Physical Development
- Creative Development.

Learning and Development

- The six areas of Learning and Development together make up the skills, knowledge and experiences appropriate for babies and children as they grow, learn and develop.
- Although these are presented as separate areas, it is important to remember that for children everything links and nothing is compartmentalised.
- The challenge for practitioners is to ensure that children's learning and development occur as an outcome of their individual interests and abilities and that planning for learning and development takes account of these

Video

There are video clips under each area of Learning and Development

Research

Independent Review of the Teaching of Early Reading [431Kb PDF]

Research Brief: A Systematic Review of the Research Literature on the Use of Phonics in the Teaching of Reading and Spelling [206Kb PDF]

Research Report: A Systematic Review of the Research Literature on the Use of Phonics in the Teaching of Reading and Spelling

Resources

Association for Physical Education

Booktouch [1143Kb PDF]

Department for Children, Schools and Families

Clicking on an area of Learning and Development provides practitioners with detailed information about the content of each aspect and what this means for children.

KEY MESSAGES CARD 4.4 (summary)

- The six areas of Learning and Development together make up the skills, knowledge and experiences appropriate for babies and children as they grow, learn and develop.
- Although these are presented as separate areas, it is important to remember that for children everything links and nothing is compartmentalised.
- The challenge for practitioners is to ensure that children's learning and development occur as an outcome of their individual interests and abilities and that planning for learning and development takes account of these.

Each area of Learning and Development is divided into aspects.

The aspects for each area are:

Personal, Social and Emotional Development
- Dispositions and Attitudes
- Self-confidence and Self-esteem
- Making Relationships
- Behaviour and Self-control
- Self-care
- Sense of Community.

Communication, Language and Literacy
- Language for Communication
- Language for Thinking
- Linking Sounds and Letters
- Reading
- Writing
- Handwriting.

Problem Solving, Reasoning and Numeracy
- Numbers as Labels and for Counting
- Calculating
- Shape, Space and Measures.

Knowledge and Understanding of the World
- Exploration and Investigation
- Designing and Making
- ICT
- Time
- Place
- Communities.

Physical Development
- Movement and Space
- Health and Bodily Awareness
- Using Equipment and Materials.

Creative Development
- Being Creative – Responding to Experiences, Expressing and Communicating Ideas
- Exploring Media and Materials
- Creating Music and Dance
- Developing Imagination and Imaginative Play.

LEARNING AND DEVELOPMENT

KEY REQUIREMENTS (*Statutory Framework* for the EYFS pg: 11, summary)

- **'All practitioners should, therefore, look carefully at the children in their care, consider their needs, their interests, and their stage of development and use all this information to help plan a challenging and enjoyable experience across all the areas of Learning and Development.'**

- **The Childcare Act 2006 provides for the EYFS Learning and Development requirements to comprise of three elements:**
  - **The EARLY LEARNING GOALS – the knowledge, skills and understanding which young children should have acquired by the end of the academic year in which they reach the age of five.**
  - **The EDUCATIONAL PROGRAMME – the matters, skills and processes which are required to be taught to young children.**
  - **The ASSESSMENT ARRANGEMENTS – the arrangements for assessing young children to ascertain their achievements.**

- **There are six areas covered by the early learning goals and educational programme.**

- **None of these areas of Learning and Development can be delivered in isolation from the others. All the areas must be delivered through planned, purposeful play, with a balance of adult-led and child-initiated activities.**

The flower icon tool on the CD-ROM has the facility to allow practitioners to select all stages or a specific broad Phase of Development, all or a specific Area of Learning and one or more areas of focus from Development matters; Look, Listen and Note; Effective practice, and Planning and resourcing.

The refined chart can then be used as a tool for planning and assessing. Information can be printed out or copied and pasted into planning and assessment documentation.

Below is an example of a chart with the following selected:
Broad phase of development: 40-60+ months.
Area of Learning: Creative Development.
Area of focus: Planning and resourcing.

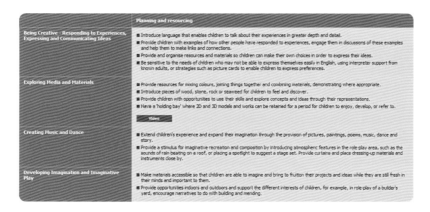

Click on the purple square to view video clips, which give examples of how the document works in practice.

A step-by-step guide to using the CD-ROM to support the observation, assessment and planning process

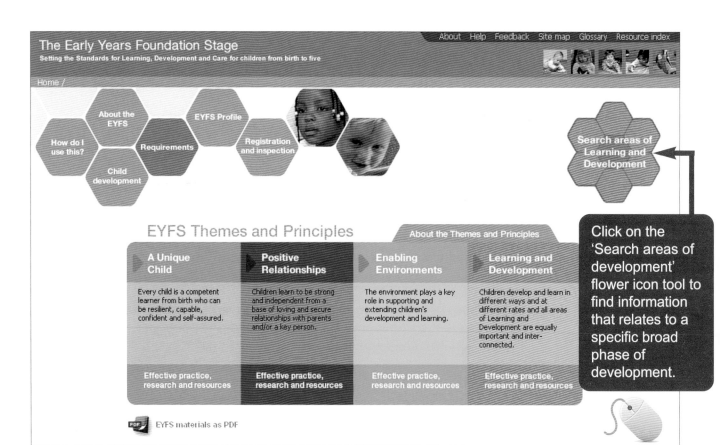

Click on the 'Search areas of development' flower icon tool to find information that relates to a specific broad phase of development.

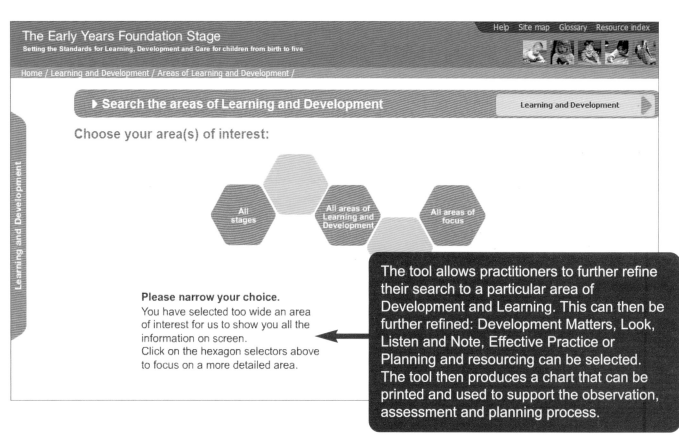

The tool allows practitioners to further refine their search to a particular area of Development and Learning. This can then be further refined: Development Matters, Look, Listen and Note, Effective Practice or Planning and resourcing can be selected. The tool then produces a chart that can be printed and used to support the observation, assessment and planning process.

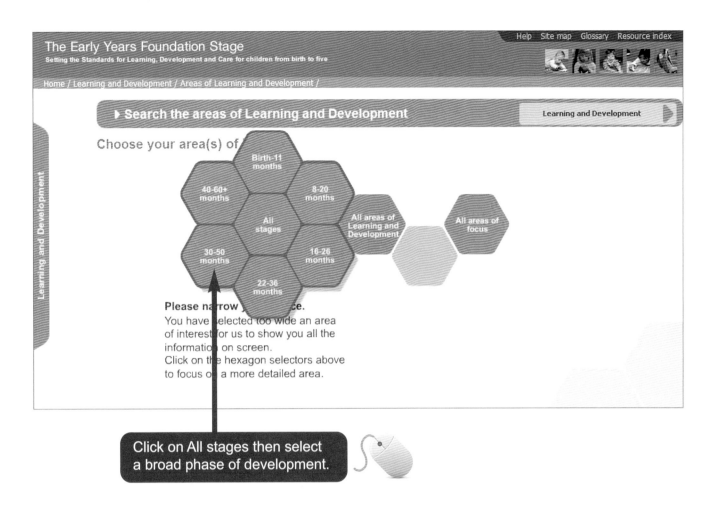

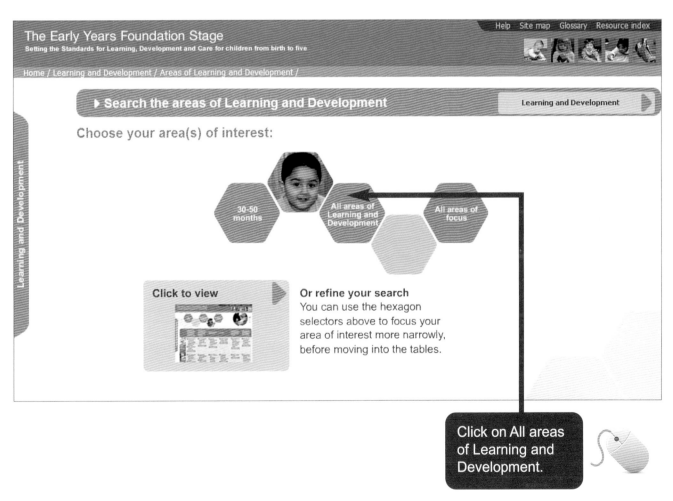

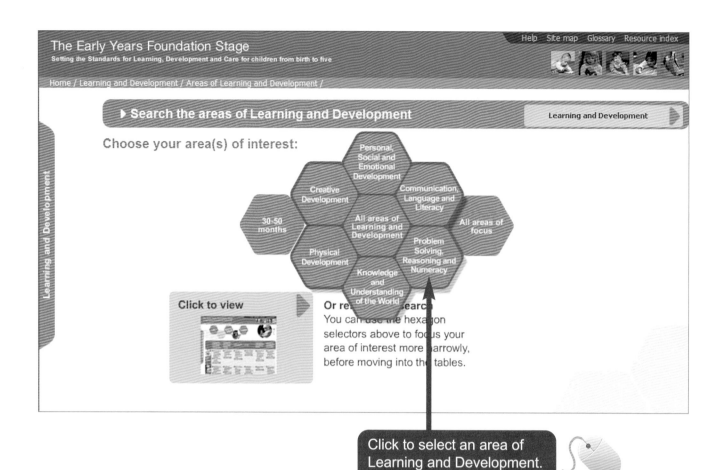

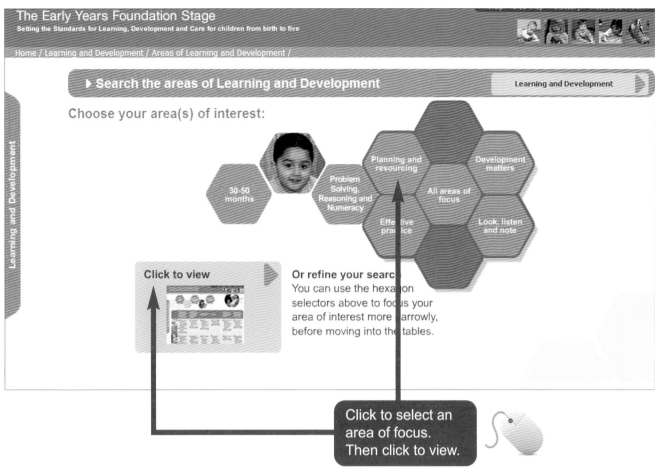

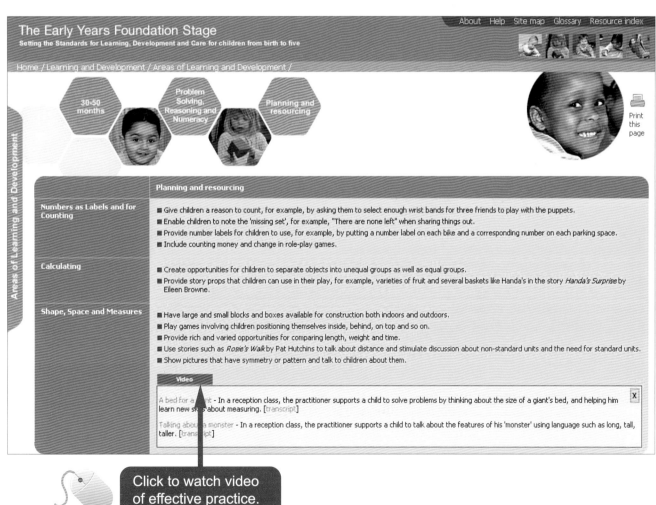

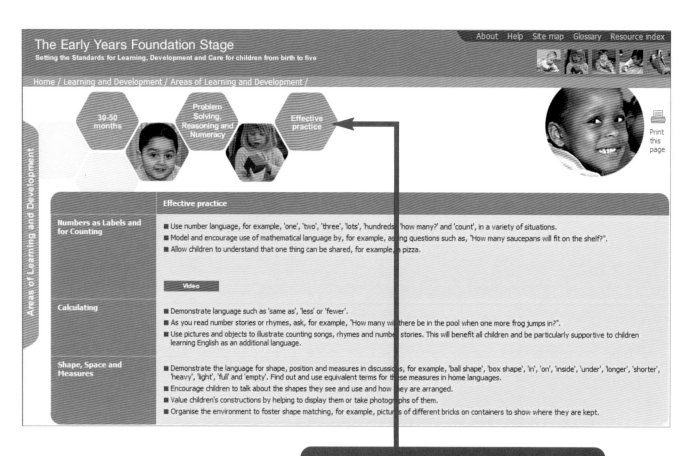

The Early Years Foundation Stage
Setting the Standards for Learning, Development and Care for children from birth to five

About   Help   Site map   Glossary   Resource index

Home / Learning and Development / Areas of Learning and Development /

30-50 months | Problem Solving, Reasoning and Numeracy | Effective practice

Print this page

Areas of Learning and Development

Effective practice

Numbers as Labels and for Counting
- Use number language, for example, 'one', 'two', 'three', 'lots', 'hundreds', 'how many?' and 'count', in a variety of situations.
- Model and encourage use of mathematical language by, for example, asking questions such as, "How many saucepans will fit on the shelf?".
- Allow children to understand that one thing can be shared, for example, a pizza.

Video

Calculating
- Demonstrate language such as 'same as', 'less' or 'fewer'.
- As you read number stories or rhymes, ask, for example, "How many will there be in the pool when one more frog jumps in?".
- Use pictures and objects to illustrate counting songs, rhymes and number stories. This will benefit all children and be particularly supportive to children learning English as an additional language.

Shape, Space and Measures
- Demonstrate the language for shape, position and measures in discussions, for example, 'ball shape', 'box shape', 'in', 'on', 'inside', 'under', 'longer', 'shorter', 'heavy', 'light', 'full' and 'empty'. Find out and use equivalent terms for these measures in home languages.
- Encourage children to talk about the shapes they see and use and how they are arranged.
- Value children's constructions by helping to display them or take photographs of them.
- Organise the environment to foster shape matching, for example, pictures of different bricks on containers to show where they are kept.

Click back on the hexagons at the top of the page to change your search. For example, you can change your focus to Effective practice or Development matters.

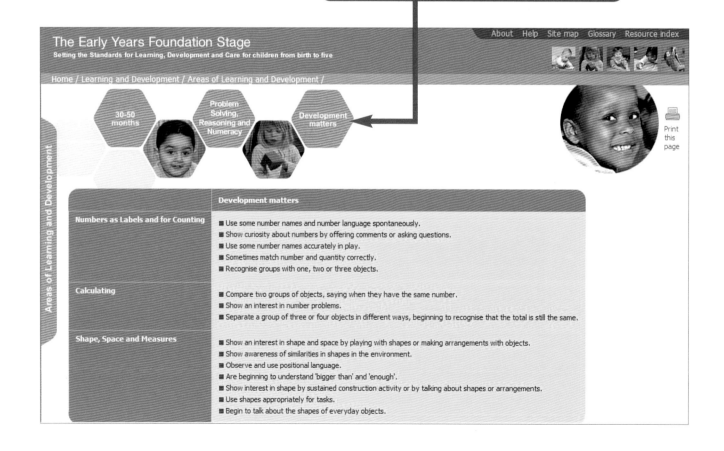

The Early Years Foundation Stage
Setting the Standards for Learning, Development and Care for children from birth to five

About   Help   Site map   Glossary   Resource index

Home / Learning and Development / Areas of Learning and Development /

30-50 months | Problem Solving, Reasoning and Numeracy | Development matters

Print this page

Areas of Learning and Development

Development matters

Numbers as Labels and for Counting
- Use some number names and number language spontaneously.
- Show curiosity about numbers by offering comments or asking questions.
- Use some number names accurately in play.
- Sometimes match number and quantity correctly.
- Recognise groups with one, two or three objects.

Calculating
- Compare two groups of objects, saying when they have the same number.
- Show an interest in number problems.
- Separate a group of three or four objects in different ways, beginning to recognise that the total is still the same.

Shape, Space and Measures
- Show an interest in shape and space by playing with shapes or making arrangements with objects.
- Show awareness of similarities in shapes in the environment.
- Observe and use positional language.
- Are beginning to understand 'bigger than' and 'enough'.
- Show interest in shape by sustained construction activity or by talking about shapes or arrangements.
- Use shapes appropriately for tasks.
- Begin to talk about the shapes of everyday objects.

Using the early support button to assist with observation, assessment and planning

The flower on the first page of the CD-ROM
enables practitioners to access additional information
which supports the early identification of special needs.

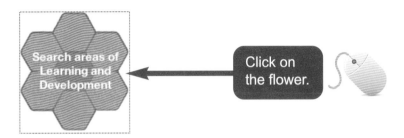

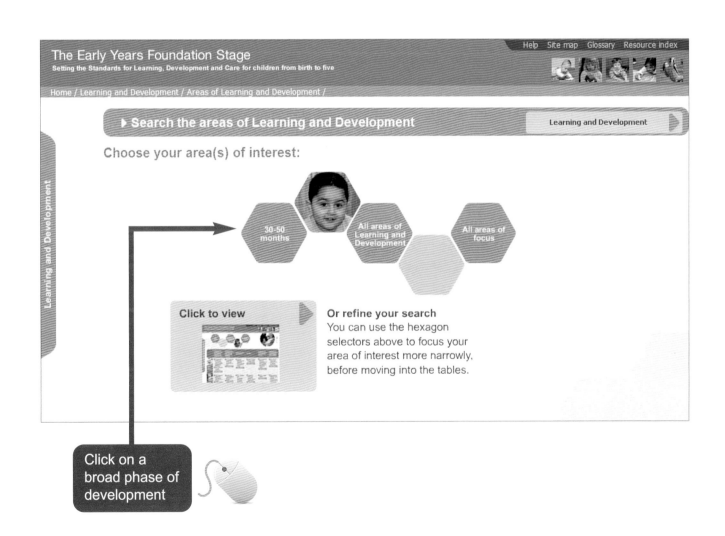

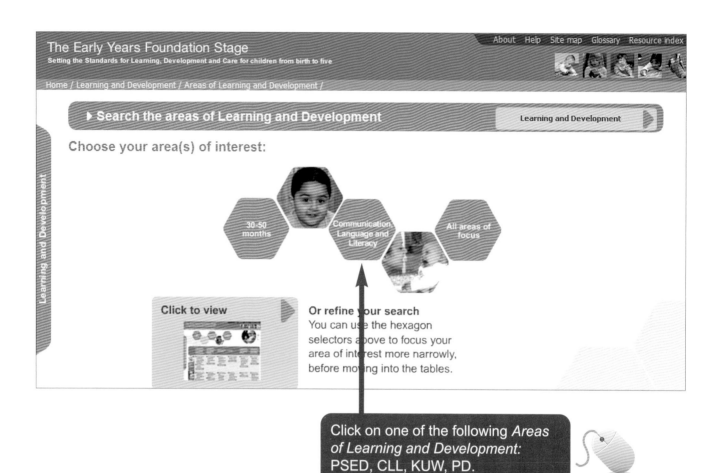

Click on one of the following *Areas of Learning and Development:* PSED, CLL, KUW, PD.

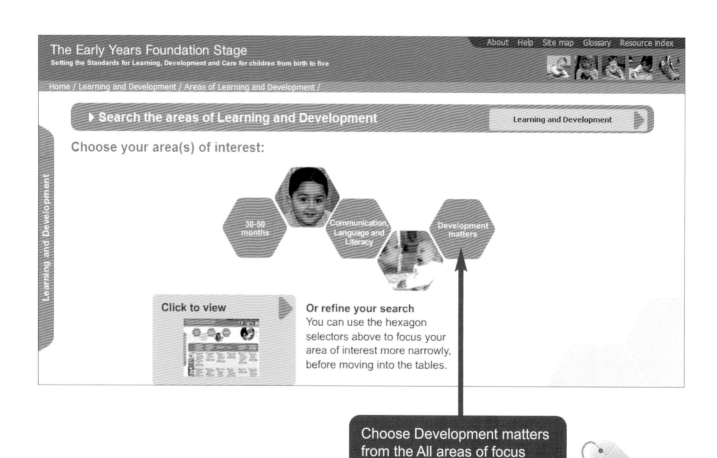

Choose Development matters from the All areas of focus hexagon, then click to view.

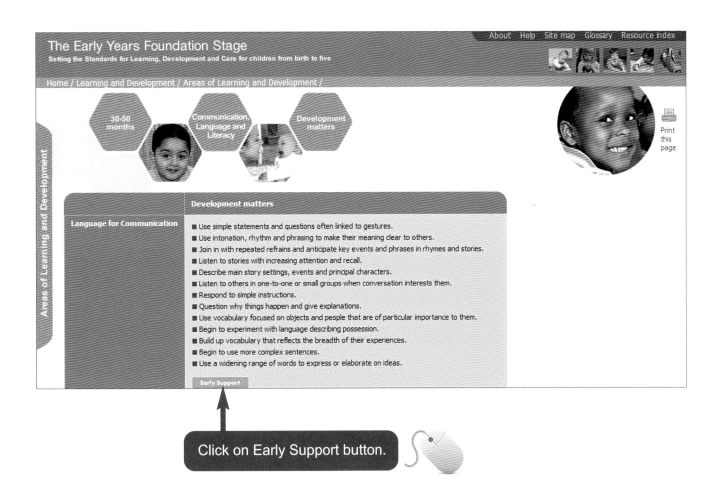

The Early Years Foundation Stage
Setting the Standards for Learning, Development and Care for children from birth to five

Home / Learning and Development / Areas of Learning and Development /

30-50 months   Communication, Language and Literacy   Development matters

Print this page

Areas of Learning and Development

Development matters

Language for Communication

- Use simple statements and questions often linked to gestures.
- Use intonation, rhythm and phrasing to make their meaning clear to others.
- Join in with repeated refrains and anticipate key events and phrases in rhymes and stories.
- Listen to stories with increasing attention and recall.
- Describe main story settings, events and principal characters.
- Listen to others in one-to-one or small groups when conversation interests them.
- Respond to simple instructions.
- Question why things happen and give explanations.
- Use vocabulary focused on objects and people that are of particular importance to them.
- Begin to experiment with language describing possession.
- Build up vocabulary that reflects the breadth of their experiences.
- Begin to use more complex sentences.
- Use a widening range of words to express or elaborate on ideas.

Early Support

Click on Early Support button.

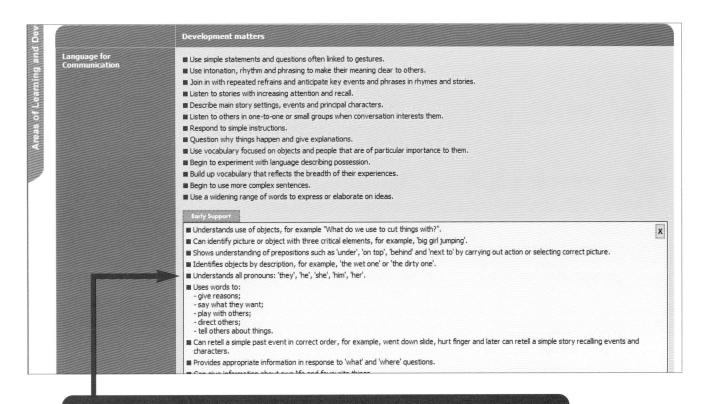

Areas of Learning and Dev

Development matters

Language for Communication

- Use simple statements and questions often linked to gestures.
- Use intonation, rhythm and phrasing to make their meaning clear to others.
- Join in with repeated refrains and anticipate key events and phrases in rhymes and stories.
- Listen to stories with increasing attention and recall.
- Describe main story settings, events and principal characters.
- Listen to others in one-to-one or small groups when conversation interests them.
- Respond to simple instructions.
- Question why things happen and give explanations.
- Use vocabulary focused on objects and people that are of particular importance to them.
- Begin to experiment with language describing possession.
- Build up vocabulary that reflects the breadth of their experiences.
- Begin to use more complex sentences.
- Use a widening range of words to express or elaborate on ideas.

Early Support   X

- Understands use of objects, for example "What do we use to cut things with?".
- Can identify picture or object with three critical elements, for example, 'big girl jumping'.
- Shows understanding of prepositions such as 'under', 'on top', 'behind' and 'next to' by carrying out action or selecting correct picture.
- Identifies objects by description, for example, 'the wet one' or 'the dirty one'.
- Understands all pronouns: 'they', 'he', 'she', 'him', 'her'.
- Uses words to:
  - give reasons;
  - say what they want;
  - play with others;
  - direct others;
  - tell others about things.
- Can retell a simple past event in correct order, for example, went down slide, hurt finger and later can retell a simple story recalling events and characters.
- Provides appropriate information in response to 'what' and 'where' questions.
- Can give information about own life and favourite things

The Early Support information gives practical examples of what practitioners might observe children doing while they are playing and interacting with other children and adults. This additional information can support in the early identification of special needs. Click on the grey cross on the top right corner of the Early Support information to hide it from your screen.

Notes

Using the self-evaluation checklists

Using the self-evaluation checklist

The self-evaluation checklist is designed to be used as a tool to support you in understanding and evaluating your delivery of the EYFS. It also supports you in planning how you can develop your practice further to effectively meet the requirements of the EYFS framework.

The EYFS brings together and simplifies the learning and development and welfare requirements between birth-to-three and three-to-five provision, allowing for continuity from birth-to five.

The checklist should be used in conjunction with the EYFS pack, which contains the *Statutory Framework*, *Practice Guidance*, Principles into Practice cards, wall poster and CD-ROM.

The *Statutory Framework* document is split into four sections.

- **Section 1** – An introduction, setting out the purposes, aims and context of the EYFS.

- **Section 2** – The requirements for learning and development.

- **Section 3** – The legal requirements and statutory guidance for the welfare requirements.

- **Section 4** – Other information, including inspection and regulation.

In section three (the welfare requirements) the legal requirements are shown under the heading 'specific legal requirements' and these *must* be complied with. The statutory guidance is shown under the heading 'statutory guidance to which providers should have regard'.

The *Practice Guidance* document is split into three sections, which provide guidance for practitioners on meeting the requirements of the EYFS framework. It aims to provide useful advice and detailed information on supporting children's learning and development and welfare.

- **Section 1** – Implementing the EYFS.

- **Section 2** – Learning and Development.

- **Section 3** – Welfare requirements.

Terminology

The term 'early years provider' refers to: maintained schools, independent schools and childcare registered by Ofsted on the Early Years Register (which was introduced in September 2008). However, where reference is made to 'Registered providers', this does not apply to schools.

Most requirements are applicable to all types of setting so that wherever parents send their children, they can be assured that essential standards of provision are in place. Some requirements, however, only apply to registered providers and therefore not to schools. Where a requirement refers only to registered providers this will be because it is either not relevant to a school or because there will be an assumption that this is already covered within a school's policies and procedures.

Ratios

The ratio requirements set out the minimum numbers of staff that must be present with the children at any time. It may, according to circumstance, be necessary to exceed these minimum requirements. The provider should consider at all times whether there is adequate supervision of children to ensure that the needs of the individual children being cared for are met. Please refer to pages 49, 50 and 51 of the *Statutory Framework* for further details and specific numbers.

How to use the self-evaluation checklist

If you work as part of an early years team it is advantageous to work through the checklist together, sharing your experiences and ideas and looking at how you can develop the EYFS further in practice. This should be seen as a working document that is revisited and re-evaluated as your practice develops.

Examples

A UNIQUE CHILD
1.1 Child Development

Issues for consideration	What are you currently doing to support this?	How could this be further developed?
Do you have a good understanding of the growth, development and learning needs of children from 0-5 years?	*Within team we have a range of experience working within the birth-to-five age range. Most experience is with three- to five-year olds where we feel fairly confident in our understanding of development and learning needs. All of team have accessed section on child development from CD-ROM and we cross reference our observations and evaluations with the Development matters section in each of the six areas of learning.*	*Access further child development training next term to cover full range from birth to five years. Meet weekly to share learning needs identified within groups.*

THE WELFARE REQUIREMENTS
Suitable premises, environment and equipment

Issues for consideration	Where can I find more information?	What are you currently doing to support this?	Next steps
Is your outdoor and indoor environment safe and suitable for your children?	Statutory Guidance, page 33, 34.	*I carry out risk assessments at the beginning of term looking at our indoor and outdoor areas and equipment that will be used. This is recorded and kept in our Health and Safety file.* *Health and Safety policy in place. All of team aware of need to keep premises and equipment clean and safe.*	*Involve all of team in procedure for carrying out risk assessment and discuss outcomes with team.* *Discuss with children keeping premises clean and safe and involve them in carrying this out. Identify when we may be able to involve children in risk assessment and how we will organise this.* *Ensure all of team have read and understand Health and Safety policy – To be completed by – date.*

Checklist to implement
the welfare requirements

THE WELFARE REQUIREMENTS
Safeguarding and promoting children's welfare

Issues for consideration	Where can I find more information?	What are you currently doing to support this?	Next steps
Do you/your setting have an effective Safeguarding Children policy and procedure in place?	*Statutory Framework*, page 22.		
Do all practitioners in the early years team have an up-to-date understanding of safeguarding issues and are able to implement the safeguarding policy and procedures?	*Statutory Framework*, page 22.		
Do you have systems in place for providing parents with information and handling complaints?	*Statutory Framework*, page 23.		
Do you maintain a regular two-way flow of information with parents and any other involved provider who collects child regularly?	*Statutory Framework*, page 23.		
Are your premises, both indoors and outdoors, safe and secure?	*Statutory Framework*, page 24.		
Do you carry out risk assessments for all outings and obtain written parental permission?	*Statutory Framework*, page 24.		
Are you obtaining and using appropriate records for outings?	*Statutory Framework*, page 24.		

THE WELFARE REQUIREMENTS
Safeguarding and promoting children's welfare – *continued*

Issues for consideration	Where can I find more information?	What are you currently doing to support this?	Next steps
Do you have and are you implementing an effective equal opportunities policy?	*Statutory Framework*, page 25.		
Are you promoting the good health of the children, taking steps to prevent spread of infection and taking appropriate action when they are ill?	*Statutory Framework*, page 26.		
Do you have an effective policy on administering medicines?	*Statutory Framework*, page 26.		
Do you know procedures to be followed in the event of injury/accident?	*Statutory Framework*, page 26.		
Are meals, snacks and drinks that you provide healthy, balanced and nutritious?	*Statutory Framework*, page 27.		
Are children in a smoke-free environment?	*Statutory Framework*, page 27.		
Do you manage children's behaviour effectively and in a manner that is appropriate for their stage of development and particular needs?	*Statutory Framework*, page 28.		

THE WELFARE REQUIREMENTS
Suitable people

Issues for consideration	Where can I find more information?	What are you currently doing to support this?	Next steps
Are all adults who are looking after children or having unsupervised access to them, suitable to do so?	*Statutory Framework*, pages 29, 30.		
Do all adults looking after children have appropriate qualifications, training, skills and knowledge?	*Statutory Framework*, page 31.		
Are your staffing arrangements organised to ensure safety and to meet the needs of your children?	*Statutory Framework*, page 32.		

THE WELFARE REQUIREMENTS
Suitable premises, environment and equipment

Issues for consideration	Where can I find more information?	What are you currently doing to support this?	Next steps
Is your outdoor and indoor environment safe and suitable for your children?	*Statutory Framework*, pages 33, 34.		

THE WELFARE REQUIREMENTS
Organisation

Issues for consideration	Where can I find more information?	What are you currently doing to support this?	Next steps
Do you plan and organise your systems to ensure that every child receives an enjoyable and challenging learning and development experience, tailored to their individual needs?	*Statutory Framework*, page 37.		

Checklist to implement the theme:
A Unique Child

A UNIQUE CHILD
1.1 Child Development

Issues for consideration	What are you currently doing to support this?	How could this be further developed?
Do you have a good understanding of the growth, development and learning needs of children from birth to five years old?		
Do you identify and build on individual interests and experiences?		
Do experiences in your setting cater for a range of learning styles and communication styles? How are you supporting each child's individual development?		
What information do you gather to obtain an accurate picture of each child and how do you keep this information up-to-date?		
How are parents involved in this process?		

A UNIQUE CHILD
1.2 Inclusive practice

Issues for consideration	What are you currently doing to support this?	How could this be further developed?
How do you reflect and celebrate diversity within your setting? In what ways are you promoting inclusion of as wide a range of children and families as possible?		
In what ways can you encourage children to recognise their own individual qualities and the characteristics they share with other children?		
How do you ensure that everyone working in your setting shares a collective responsibility for inclusion?		

A UNIQUE CHILD
1.3 Keeping Safe

Issues for consideration	What are you currently doing to support this?	How could this be further developed?
What systems are in place to ensure that children are safe and protected in terms of physical and psychological well-being?		
How are you helping children to learn to assess risk?		
What opportunities are there for children to make choices?		
How do you ensure children understand boundaries?		
How do you ensure that children experience challenge at an appropriate level for each individual?		
What experiences in your setting help children to think about keeping themselves safe?		

A UNIQUE CHILD
1.4 Health and Well-being

Issues for consideration	What are you currently doing to support this?	How could this be further developed?
What opportunities are there for children to choose to be physically active throughout the day?		
What opportunities are there for children to rest when needed?		
How do you help children to feel good about themselves?		
How are you creating an emotionally supportive environment?		
Is your environment physically comfortable for all children throughout the day?		
Do experiences fit with the children's rhythms allowing for flexibility?		

Checklist to implement the theme:
Positive Relationships

POSITIVE RELATIONSHIPS
2.1 Respecting Each Other

Issues for consideration	What are you currently doing to support this?	How could this be further developed?
Do you encourage children to express their range of emotions?		
How do you respond to outbursts so that children understand that their behaviour does not threaten their relationship with us?		
How do you encourage collaborative play?		
Are children given the opportunity to choose who they wish to be with?		
Do you value and support children's friendships?		
Within the early years team are you modelling respectful relationships?		

POSITIVE RELATIONSHIPS
2.2 Parents as Partners

Issues for consideration	What are you currently doing to support this?	How could this be further developed?
Do all families using your setting feel valued and welcome?		
Do you use a wide range of ways to communicate with parents and families?		
Do you communicate regularly with parents and is this effective two-way communication?		
Do you use information from parents to inform planning for their child? How do you encourage the involvement of fathers in the setting?		

POSITIVE RELATIONSHIPS
2.3 Supporting Learning

Issues for consideration	What are you currently doing to support this?	How could this be further developed?
Do you provide a rich, sensory environment?		
Do you tune into children rather than talking at them?		
Do you take lead and direction from the child?		
Do you encourage and extend curiosity?		
Do you help children to make connections in their learning?		
Do you help children to reflect on their learning?		
Do you plan for both child- and adult-initiated experiences?		
Do you have a balance of adult roles to focus children's experiences and to support and provide an overview of experiences?		

POSITIVE RELATIONSHIPS
2.4 Key Person

Issues for consideration	What are you currently doing to support this?	How could this be further developed?
Has each child an assigned key person?		
Does the key person support the child settling in and help develop their confidence?		
Does the key person liaise with parents regularly to share information about their child?		
Does the key person support the child at times of transition and in new or unfamiliar situations?		
Does the key person know his/her key children well and is he/she developing a relationship with them?		
Does the key person provide security, comfort and support?		

Checklist to implement the theme:
Enabling Environments

ENABLING ENVIRONMENTS
3.1 Observation, Assessment and Planning

Issues for consideration	What are you currently doing to support this?	How could this be further developed?
Do you use participant, incidental and planned observations on a regular basis for each child?		
Do you use a range of evidence to record your observations?		
Do you analyse and review each child's development and learning?		
Do your observations inform your planning?		
Are you planning for individual needs using information from observations?		
Does your long-term and medium-term planning support you in covering all six areas of Learning and Development and the principles of the EYFS?		

ENABLING ENVIRONMENTS
3.1 *continued*

Issues for consideration	What are you currently doing to support this?	How could this be further developed?
Does your long-term planning show a balance of indoor and outdoor learning?		
Is your short-term planning informed by your observations from the previous day and previous week?		
Are you able to focus on individual specific needs and how these will be met?		
If you use theme-based planning, is the theme very broad, flexible and child lead?		

ENABLING ENVIRONMENTS
3.2 Supporting Every Child

Issues for consideration	What are you currently doing to support this?	How could this be further developed?
Do you provide a variety of learning experiences to cater for different learning styles?		
Is the environment flexible and varied enough to respect and respond to individual needs?		
Do you provide opportunities for children to work together with an adult, a peer, in a group or individually?		
Do you provide both familiar and new experiences so that children can feel both reassured and stimulated and extended?		
Do you personalise support for individual children, building on their strengths and interests?		
Do you involve children in planning as far as possible so that you can incorporate their ideas?		
Are you aware of, and responding to, the uniqueness of each child's experience, development and learning?		

ENABLING ENVIRONMENTS
3.3 The Learning Environment

Issues for consideration	What are you currently doing to support this?	How could this be further developed?
Do you create an emotionally warm and accepting environment?		
Do children feel confident to express their emotions?		
Do you use praise and encouragement to raise children's self-esteem and confidence?		
Do you have a balance between indoor and outdoor learning?		
Does your outdoor environment provide different learning experiences to those provided indoors? Is your environment well organised to promote independence and appropriate challenge?		

Issues for consideration	What are you currently doing to support this?	How could this be further developed?
Do you know the pattern of each child's day? (e.g. childminder, breakfast club, after school club, nursery)		
Do you share information from other settings to inform your records and planning?		
Are you communicating with other services to achieve the *Every Child Matters* outcomes? (e.g. Speech therapist)		
Do you develop partnerships with other childcare providers and community groups or individuals in your area? (e.g. local artist)		

Checklist to implement the theme:
Learning and Development

Issues for consideration	What are you currently doing to support this?	How could this be further developed?
The EYFS is a play-based curriculum: is this reflected in your planning and practice?		
Are children able to spend extended time in self-chosen play and exploration?		
Are children able to direct and lead their play even when an adult is supporting them?		
Do you use contexts for play taken from children's own day-to-day experiences? (e.g. popular culture)		
Do children have the opportunity for first-hand experiences whenever possible? (e.g. real minibeast rather than plastic replica)		

LEARNING AND DEVELOPMENT
4.2 Active Learning

Issues for consideration	What are you currently doing to support this?	How could this be further developed?
Do you provide opportunities for children to practice and repeat new skills in a variety of different situations?		
Do you plan for choice and decision-making in activities?		
Do you provide a range of activities and resources to ensure that each child in your group can find something that will engage and sustain their interest?		
Do you annotate your planning to cater for individual needs and interests?		

LEARNING AND DEVELOPMENT
4.3 Creativity and Critical Thinking

Issues for consideration	What are you currently doing to support this?	How could this be further developed?
Do you provide opportunities for children to connect their ideas in a variety of ways through movement, dance, painting and imaginative play?		
Do you focus on the process rather than the end product in creative experiences? (e.g. Are all children expected to use the same materials in the same way to make the same festival card?)		
Do you encourage children to talk about their learning?		
Do you pose questions to extend children's critical thinking?		
Does your environment inspire children to be creative and to rethink ideas?		
Do you create a flexible environment offering open-ended resources?		

LEARNING AND DEVELOPMENT
4.4 Areas of Learning and Development

Issues for consideration	What are you currently doing to support this?	How could this be further developed?
Does children's learning and development occur as an outcome of their individual interests and abilities?		
Does your planning and practice reflect a balance between the six areas of Learning and Development?		
Do the experiences you offer combine and link the areas of Learning and Development, rather than focusing on them as separate experiences?		
Do you use information gathered from observations and assessments to inform your planning?		
Does your daily routine provide a balance of adult-led, adult-directed and child-initiated learning opportunities?		

Notes

Notes